'Here's my secret: sometimes, when I hear all kinds of outrageous things said and done in the name of Christianity, I think about turning in my membership. I don't want to be part of the elite club of the doctrinally correct and the spiritually superior. But then a book like this one comes along, and I say, "This is a way of being a Christian that makes sense to me. This is a way of life I can live with." I'm glad to be known as a bad Christian, thanks to Dave Tomlinson and this beautiful book.'
Brian D. McLaren, author of *Why Did Jesus, Moses, the Buddha, and Mohammed Cross the Road?*

'In view of what Dave Tomlinson says about religion and conventional church life, I do hope that a commendation from his Bishop will not put people off reading a book that is so rich in humanity and written by someone who is a convincing and compassionate pastor – but possibly not a very good member of the Deanery Synod.'

Richard Chartres, Bishop of London

'A vicar in the pub is worth two in a pulpit. Dave Tomlinson's *How to be a bad Christian* is as welcome as a glistening pint to a thirsty patron. Free from religious claptrap and moralistic badgering, here's a book that talks about God without boring your socks off. Tomlinson allows humanity and grace to escape the shackles of pious pedants, and flow into the world we all inhabit. Beautifully written, full of streetwise stories and wisdom, delightful and engaging – read it and discover how good it is to be among the bad. A rip-snorting manifesto for a way of living that makes a difference in the world.'

Mike Riddell, author of *The Insatiable Moon*

'Dave is super-intelligent, funny, passionate, encouraging, generous, hard-working, self-giving, creative and a deeply faithful witness to the love of God – in short, a bad Christian. His book is a great gift to all who are searching for abundant life, in and out of church.'

Sara Miles, author of *Take This Bread* and *Jesus Freak*

'Dave Tomlinson is superb priest who is driven by God's love in Christ, and who understands the spiritual instincts and needs of ordinary people. But he has to work within – or against – an institutional church that too often either cannot communicate at all, or else communicates a false God with a repellent face. If the Christian faith is ever to capture the imagination of our culture, we have to learn the lessons of this book.'

Jeffrey John, Dean of St Albans

'This is a wonderful, wise and perceptive book by a man who understands what's going on in the hearts and minds of the millions of us who have given up on church, but can't give up on the idea of God. It's warm and witty at the same time as being honest and profound. Reading it will help you understand what's really happening to spirituality in this country, which is more exciting and full of possibility than most of us know. More than that, it will help you understand what's going on in your own soul.'

Cole Moreton, author and journalist

'When I read books by Dave Tomlinson, I find myself wanting to kiss their pages. *How to be a bad Christian* is no exception. This book is for anyone who's ever thought that being a person of faith means you must shut down your intellect and become priggish. If all vicars, ministers, priests and pastors had Dave's compassionate wisdom and his unconditional, radical inclusivity, our churches would be bursting at the seams ... and perhaps Ghandi might never have said "Your Christians are so unlike your Christ." I aspire to be a really bad Christian.'

Karla Yaconelli

'Tomlinson writes as a parish priest with a pastoral heart for his community – an increasingly rare combination in these days of CEO-led churches. He puts the "pastor" back in "pastoral" and the "mission" back in "missional" as he describes his understanding of contemporary ministry at the interface of the institutional church and the community outside it. He wants the people he meets in pew and pub to understand the hope that following Jesus brings. His perspectives are compassionate, engaging, and refreshing. He's not afraid to expose elephant after elephant sitting in the pews of every church. Any person training for pastoral leadership should read this, as should anyone who is struggling with understanding what loving and being loved by God was intended to be like.'

Mark Pierson, pastor, worship curator, author

'I am a bad Christian! – and it's wonderfully reassuring to know that God still loves me. Dave's tapped into what God's love really means, and how we can all embrace it in our lives – which will in turn spill out into the community. Be kind to yourself and read this book: it made me laugh and cry in equal measure.'

Janey Lee Grace, author of *Look Great Naturally*

'Where is God? It's a question I often ask people. Does God live in church? Does God live in Christianity? Does God live in the world and everything we know? In Dave Tomlinson's book *How to be a bad Christian* we wander through paths of discovery to find that God is wherever God wants to be. This is a gentle yet profound book, which nudges people towards receptivity through stories and reflections. It invites us to imagine that the "spirit blows where the Spirit wills", and through its stories we are invited into a generous orthodoxy of faith where people discover their humanity – through discovering God, themselves, and an accepting love. Bad becomes good and good becomes reimagined. Please read it: it could change our communities, and the world.'

Fuzz Kitto, international church consultant

How to be a bad Christian

...And a better human being

Dave Tomlinson

With illustrations by Rob Pepper

HODDER &
STOUGHTON

Unless indicated otherwise, Scripture quotations are taken from the
Holy Bible, New Revised Standard Version (Anglicised edition).
Copyright 1989 by the Division of Christian Education of the
National Council of the Churches of Christ in the USA. Used by permission.

Scripture quotations marked *The Message* are taken from *The Message* translation.
Copyright © 1993, 1994, 1995, 1996, 2000, 2001, 2002.
Used by permission of NavPress Publishing Group.

First published in Great Britain in 2012 by Hodder & Stoughton
An Hachette UK company

2

Copyright © Dave Tomlinson, 2012
Illustrations copyright © Rob Pepper, 2012

The right of Dave Tomlinson to be identified as the Author
of the Work has been asserted by him in accordance with
the Copyright, Designs and Patents Act 1988.

A CIP catalogue record for this title is available from the British Library

ISBN 978 1 444 70382 5
eBook ISBN 978 1 444 70384 9

Typeset in Sabon MT by Hewer Text UK Ltd, Edinburgh

Printed and bound in the UK by CPI Group (UK) Ltd, Croydon CR0 4YY

Hodder & Stoughton policy is to use papers that are natural, renewable
and recyclable products and made from wood grown in sustainable forests.
The logging and manufacturing processes are expected to conform to
the environmental regulations of the country of origin.

Hodder & Stoughton Ltd
338 Euston Road
London NW1 3BH

www.hodderfaith.com

For my grandchildren,
Gracie, Zoe & Jude

Contents

Acknowledgements ix

1. God without the guff
   how to keep faith and ditch religion 1

2. Bumping into God
   how to find God without going near a church 13

3. It's all you need!
   how to love your way to heaven 23

4. It's not about the rules
   how to think with your soul 35

5. Wakey! Wakey!
   how to make sure you live before you die 49

6. Dumping the guilt trip
   how to forgive yourself and move on 63

7. Laughing with God
   how to get to heaven by having a good time 75

8. Change what you can
   how to dump bad choices and make good ones 85

9. God is not a Christian
   how to appreciate other religions
   without losing your own   97

10. Never mind heaven, what about now?
    how to be at home in this world   109

11. Good God/bad God?
    how to make sense of suffering   121

12. A wing and a prayer
    how to talk to God   135

13. Did God write anything else?
    how to read the Bible and other good books   145

14. Knock down the walls!
    how to make church for everyone   161

15. The quiet revolution
    how to help God change the world   173

16. It's over to you!
    how to be the person you were born to be   189

17. The last word
    how to be a bad Christian   203

    Appendix 1: Spiritual practices   209
    Appendix 2: The Enneagram   218
    Appendix 3: Useful websites   224

Acknowledgements

To my wife Pat, who is my greatest supporter and my most trusted critic, who also took on a great deal of extra work to enable me to get this book written. To my children Jeni, Paul and Lissy, and their partners Paul, Cyndi and Andrée, for their love and endless belief in me. To Rob Pepper for his lovely illustrations and for being my pal and encourager. To Katherine Venn my editor for her friendship and hugely appreciated input that made this a better book than it would otherwise have been. To the St Luke's community for their love and friendship, and to the people of Holloway who provided me with wonderful stories. To my friend and colleague Martin Wroe for his eternal optimism and inspiration. Also, thanks to Andrew and Sibylle Harrison for lovingly badgering me to get this book written. And to all the staff at Hodder Faith who believed in this venture and brought it to magnificent fruition with skill and excitement.

Thank you one and all. I owe you!

A Christian is one who is on the way, though not necessarily very far along it, and who has at least some dim and half-baked idea of whom to thank.

Frederick Buechner

1. God without the guff
how to keep faith and ditch religion

Every day people are straying away from the Church and going back to God.

– Lenny Bruce

It was a cold, damp Thursday in mid-February. A good day for a funeral, some might say. The church was jammed with mourners, standing room only, gathered to bid farewell to a larger-than-life seventy-three-year-old Islington man known as 'Fast Eddie'.

1

After a moving service, punctuated with tears and laughter, we left the church and travelled to the crematorium for the committal. A few cars carrying important family members got lost on the way, so proceedings were held up. Most people took refuge from the biting wind in the crematorium chapel, where the atmosphere was surprisingly upbeat for a funeral – but then, we had been warned that Eddie wanted no glum faces. Apparently he told his wife, 'If anyone starts bawling, I'll come back to bloody haunt them!'

So, yes, most people tried to honour his wishes. Eddie wasn't someone you would want haunting you.

Waiting for the latecomers, and chatting with the funeral director at the front of the chapel, I was approached by Eddie's niece who had with her in a car seat her three-month-old baby. 'This is Arthur,' she said. 'Would you bless him, please, Dave?'

'What, now?' I replied.

'Yeah, whenever,' she said.

So right there in the crematorium for all to see, I cradled little Arthur in my arms and said a blessing over him, tracing the mark of the cross on his tiny, silky forehead. Cameras flashed. Mum and Dad beamed. Grandparents looked on proudly. The congregation applauded. The organist looked baffled. And Arthur gazed up at me, no idea what was going on or where he was, but looking perfectly at peace with the whole thing.

'Bloody hell, Dave!' the funeral director said. 'I've never seen anything like this before! This is definitely a first on me.'

'Eddie would have loved it,' someone said. Everyone agreed.

Eddie's funeral took up most of that day. And while it's always sad to be the one hitting the button at the crematorium, triggering that final surge of emotion as the coffin slides away, it was one of my more satisfying days – being a priest to a part of God's family who mostly don't appear in church, but who are God's family all the same.

The conversations in the pub afterwards were the sort I often have with people who don't go to church. I lose count of the times folk say to me, apologetically, 'I'm not a very good Christian . . .'

The underlying guilt in the statement disturbs me. Where does it come from? These are fine people, whom I like and respect and enjoy spending time with. I find no substantial difference between them and the people who appear in church every Sunday. Are they less decent human beings? Do they love their children less, or try less strenuously or sincerely to make good choices in life? Of course not!

So I often say, 'Well, I'm a bad Christian too!' At which point they pull back, eyes wide open with shock. Or they smile. Or giggle at the idea of a vicar admitting that he's a bad Christian.

Michael, one of Fast Eddie's friends, actually apologised to me that he didn't come to church. 'No need to apologise,' I replied. 'Most people don't come to church. But if I thought for one moment that God gave a monkey's fart whether or not you come to church, I'd become an atheist here and now!'

Ironically, the upshot of this conversation was that Michael did turn up at church the following week.

Don't get me wrong: I think there are good reasons to be part of a church community, which we'll get to later in the book. But I cannot believe that God divides the world between churchgoers and non-churchgoers, or between people who believe and people who don't believe. What an absurd idea. Surely God has more sophistication to his judgement than this! Surely God has to be more interested in the kind of people we are, the choices we make in life and the way we treat people than in what we do with our Sunday mornings?

I know from untold conversations with the sort of people who attended Eddie's funeral that there is no shortage of spiritual insight and sensitivity in the lives of folk who never darken the doors of a church. Plenty of people mull over the meaning of life – while lying awake in bed at night, or over a couple of pints of beer in the pub. Plenty have genuine spiritual experiences of one sort or another. Plenty have delightful theological insights – mostly expressed in refreshingly non-religious terminology.

However, very few of these people imagine that going to church will add anything significant to their lives, or provide them with any useful skills or resources for coping more effectively with life. In the minds of most non-churchgoers, religion and church are for goodie-goodies, religious nerds and Bible-bashers – or even, sadly, for people who they think are better than them.

But this doesn't mean that God is not a part of their lives, or that they are not on some sort of spiritual journey. Far from it: some of the most moving and impressive spiritual insights I encounter come from people who never go near a church or consider themselves religious. Indeed, I can't tell you how many of my sermons contain wise titbits from non-religious friends and parishioners.

There is also a common misconception that being a Christian means you have to believe certain things – give the nod to a pile of religious ideas and theories. This is simply not so. Beliefs are important; I have lots of them. But I don't think any of my beliefs are going to get me into heaven – or keep me out! I can't see St Peter standing at the Pearly Gates with a clipboard checking up on people's beliefs. Jesus himself made no requirement that people subscribe to particular doctrines before becoming his followers. But he did call on people to change their ways: to stop being greedy, to become peacemakers, to love their enemies and so on. Jesus never wrote a book, never created a creed, never started a church and never intended to begin a new religion. He simply demonstrated the way of love – the golden rule in any religious tradition – and invited people to join him in that.

Jesus certainly didn't invent the term 'Christian', which actually appears only three times in the entire Bible. It was probably originally devised by critics of Christ's followers, at least a decade after his death, as a term of derision. But it stuck – for better or worse.

Before they took the name 'Christian', early followers of Christ were simply known as 'people of the way' – people who identified with the way of life Jesus taught and demonstrated. I like that, 'people of the way'. It suggests being part of a journey, rather than part of an organisation. And I know lots of people who never turn up at church, who struggle with creeds and doctrines, who shrink from the thought of being religious, yet who are very much in the way of Christ. They would deny being Christians. But they are lying through their teeth! They are people of the way – 'bad Christians' through and through.

Let's get it clear: Christianity is about faith, not belief. There is a difference. Faith is about having trust, whereas belief is more akin to having opinions. It's possible to hold beliefs passionately and to argue about them until the cows come home, without them making a scrap of difference to us. But trust is not about beliefs, creeds, opinions, arguments; it's more instinctive, more fundamental. It doesn't need words. It's in your belly.

Carol is someone I spent time talking with in the pub after Eddie's funeral. It's amazing what people tell you just because you're wearing a dog collar and seem half-human. As she told me about the abusive marriage she escaped from a couple of years before, I couldn't believe her story. Barely avoiding weeping into my beer glass, I listened to her tale of violence and brutality, of cigarettes stubbed out on her body and bruises concealed so friends and family would not know.

'I don't go to church, Dave,' she said. 'I'm not religious or anything like that. But the thing that got me through was knowing that Someone or Something was with me – God, Christ, whatever. And this voice said, "Don't worry; you'll get through this. It will stop." And it did. I don't know what it is, Dave, but I know, rock solid, that Something is there. Something got me through.'

Carol had faith – trust. Lots of it. She wasn't strong on religious patter. She couldn't use nice churchy phrases. But she had faith in some kind of loving, supporting presence that got her through. She had God without the guff!

The Spanish writer Miguel Unamuno wonderfully dramatises the difference between belief and faith in his short story 'Saint Manuel Bueno, Martyr', which tells of a young man at his mother's deathbed. With the local priest present in the room, the woman grasps her son's hand and asks him to pray for her. The son sits in silence. When he leaves the room, he tells the priest that he can't pray for his mother because he doesn't believe in God. 'That's nonsense,' the priest replies. 'You don't have to believe in God to pray.'

The sort of prayer the priest referred to – the sort of prayer the dying woman hoped for, the sort of prayer Carol offered as the punches fell – wasn't the sort of prayer from a prayer book, but the kind that comes from the gut. It's visceral, almost physical. It may seem absurd, illogical, when analysed, yet it's instinctive and irresistible. It's about having faith – not words and beliefs, but deep trust.

But what is it that we're trusting in at such times? To whom do we cry out in our need? God, yes, but not the old man with a beard in the sky. No one in their right mind believes in that sort of God any more. God is, surely, a mystery – the One who transcends everything that we humans can imagine. And yet . . .

And yet, even though we know that God isn't any kind of human being – not even Superman! – the only way we can imagine God is in personal terms. Traditionally, Christians have portrayed God as a father figure, but we can equally picture God as a mother, a loving parent, a constant presence in good times and bad, who is there for us. Often, we would like God to intervene and miraculously transform our circumstances, and occasionally something like this does seem to happen. However, more often, as Carol's story shows, God is experienced as a supporting, strengthening presence that gets us through painful circumstances.

You don't need to be religious to sense God as a loving presence in your life. Personally, I think that the Church would be far better to stop trying to pump the gospel into people's lives, and recognise that God is there already – named or unnamed. The Quakers have a wonderful way of understanding this with the idea of an 'inner light', or 'the Christ within'. They hold that there is 'that of God' within everyone, and that this has nothing to do with religion or churchgoing; it's part of being human.

I think that the word 'Christian' is much better thought of as a verb than a noun. Jesus didn't call people to wear a badge or join a club. He called them to follow him: to join him in spreading love and healing in the world. When we treat 'Christian' as a verb – a 'doing word' – instead of a noun, it changes everything. We stop saying 'I am a Christian', and start looking at how we can behave in Christian ways. The Christian faith is then seen as a spiritual practice rather than a belief system.

So what does Christianity look like as a spiritual practice rather than a belief system? That's really what the rest of this book is about. For now, let me pinpoint just three things.

First, Christianity as a spiritual practice means learning to live in the presence of a loving God – knowing that you are never alone and that God's love for you will never run out.

Second, it means learning to make good choices – responding to life in ways that respect our deepest sense of what is right.

Third, it means learning to love our neighbour as we love our own selves – becoming givers instead of mere takers.

The sort of people who were at Fast Eddie's funeral are typical of legions of folk who are put off Christianity by all the guff and paraphernalia that has grown up around it for two thousand years.

This book is written for them, for you, for countless ordinary people who may cringe at organised religion, have little time for creeds and doctrines and churchgoing, yet nevertheless attempt, albeit falteringly, to live in the spirit of Christianity or true religion – to be in 'the way'.

So hey, if the cap fits, wear it.

Congratulations!

You're a bad Christian!

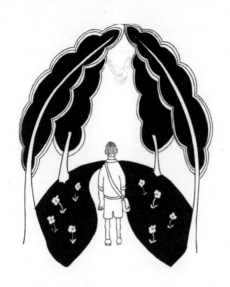

2. Bumping into God

how to find God without going near a church

The eye that sees nobility and beauty in what another would regard as ordinary is the eye of prayer.

– Sister Wendy Beckett

Holy Joes was a 'church' for bad Christians.

It met in the upstairs room of a pub in South London, and for the ten years I led the group it provided a 'no-holds-barred' opportunity for people to explore, debate and

13

argue about religion and Christianity – without anyone telling you what you were supposed to think and believe at the end of the night. There were none of the usual trappings of a church, just the space to interact and explore over a few drinks.

When Andrew first appeared at Holy Joes he announced that he was a Wiccan, and part of a pagan group called Philoso-Forum that also met in a pub in South London. He was an open-minded man with an excellent understanding of Christianity, who contributed constructively to the group. After some months he suggested that Holy Joes and Philoso-Forum meet for a dialogue. In fact, we ended up getting together on three occasions, each of which was fascinating.

During one of our meetings people from both groups talked about their first spiritual experience. Andrew spoke of an occasion when he was eleven, walking in some local woods during the summer holidays. As he paused in a glade, he was overwhelmed by a sense of oneness with everything around him – the trees and flowers, the sound of the birds, the smell of the woods. Unaccountably, he just stood there crying with joy.

When he enthusiastically told his Sunday school teacher about the experience, he talked of feeling surrounded by the spirits in the trees, the flowers and the birds. The grim-faced teacher clearly disapproved, telling the young boy that talk of spirits in nature was pagan, and dangerous.

Andrew didn't go to church after this. But, ironically, he eventually became a pagan. Reflecting on the experience, he said that had his teacher encouraged him to understand the 'spirits' as the presence of God in nature, he would probably still be a Christian.

Andrew bumped into God in the woods – in a way he never did in church. And he is far from alone: many people feel closer to God in nature – or sharing a meal with friends, or watching a film, or whatever – than they do in a religious gathering.

Anyone who has seen the classic 1999 film *American Beauty* will recall the plastic bag scene. It's where the teenager Ricky asks his friend Jane if she would like to see the most beautiful thing he's ever filmed. Ricky is something of a troubled mystic who sees beauty in the minutiae of everyday life, and videos as much as he can for fear of missing it.

So they sit in front of Ricky's television to watch his cherished film: a haunting sequence of a plastic bag dancing in the wind in front of a graffitied wall. With tears in his eyes, Ricky explains, 'It was one of those days when it's a minute away from snowing and there's this

electricity in the air, you can almost hear it. And this bag
was, like, dancing with me. Like a little kid begging me to
play with it. For fifteen minutes. And that's the day I knew
there was this entire life behind things, and . . . this
incredibly benevolent force, that wanted me to know
there was no reason to be afraid . . . ever. Video's a poor
excuse, I know. But it helps me remember . . . and I need
to remember . . . Sometimes there's so much beauty in the
world I feel like I can't take it, like my heart's going to
cave in.'

What Ricky recounts and what Andrew experienced in
the woods are the kinds of mystical encounters found
within all the world's religious traditions: when a person
catches a glimpse beyond the outward world of objects
and events to get a peek of a greater reality that exists all
around and within us – 'this entire life behind things,
and . . . this incredibly benevolent force'.

Most of the time, most of us are unaware of this greater
reality behind things. We are immersed in the mundane,
preoccupied with the outward world. The interior or
spiritual dimension remains hidden; God seems absent.
Yet a mystic loiters within each of us, waiting to be
noticed and nurtured.

We all have moments when we glimpse something
beyond the purely material world, when we 'bump into

God'. But we don't necessarily think of them as religious or spiritual experiences. I'm talking about those ordinary 'sacred' moments that may be joyful, sad, inspirational, melancholic, awesome:

> receiving an underserved smile from a child;
> gazing at the Milky Way on a dark night far from city lights;
> holding the hand of a dying loved one;
> gazing at a city cleansed by a recent fall of snow;
> weeping over a broken relationship;
> sipping a cold beer on a summer day, with nothing to do;
> feeling inspired by a new project;
> hearing a blackbird sing as dusk falls in winter;
> standing at an open grave.

Life is packed with moments of God-ness, but mostly we walk by on the other side, anxious about a meeting, hurrying to catch a bus, wondering what to do tonight, dreaming about the weekend, falling asleep on the inside.

And the world is an ambiguous place, so sometimes we miss the God-experiences because we are so aware of the darkness and evil that we see, or that we hear about in the media. At its best, religion can help us not to be over-whelmed by the darkness, and even to believe that we can make some small contribution to eliminating it. Faith is a way of interpreting the world, of making sense of the God-moments as well as finding hope in the dark times.

However, increasingly, religious explanations seem hollow or outdated and irrelevant. Most of us never think to go to church, because we have no confidence that it will offer any sort of vision of God or of the universe that is compelling, or inspiring, or useful. But the questions persist – albeit frequently shoved to the back of our minds.

A while back I took the funeral of Gilbert, a two-week-old baby. After a harrowing service at the crematorium, I (yet again!) spent most of the day in the pub with seventy or so relatives and family friends. (It's always tricky navigating one's way through a day when everyone seems hell-bent on buying the vicar a drink.) Walking home several hours later, I reflected with satis-faction on the forty or so significant conversations I must have had that day.

Many of these naturally focused on the perplexing quandary of the death of a baby – trying to find the hope that I mentioned a moment ago. But once people settled that I wasn't the vague, pious figure they some-how expected a vicar to be, I was inundated with all the questions and queries they had stashed away in that file named 'Very Hard Questions That I Must Get Answers

To, One Day'.

However, the more significant conversations focused on personal questions about bereavement and broken relationships, about guilty secrets and feelings of shame. We were in a pub, not a church, but God filled the place. Towards the end of the day, the father of the deceased child said, 'I think you've found a new flock here, Dave.'

The trouble is, we have so few opportunities to open our file of difficult, unanswered questions. And our culture provides meagre speech to express or explore our spirituality in a way that isn't either horribly churchy or spookily new age.

The whole notion of 'God' is the perfect example of this. Most people have long ago discarded the idea of an old man with a long beard sitting in the heavens, but what do we put in its place? Some theologians talk of God as 'the ground of being' or the 'ultimate reality', which is fine, but too abstract for most of us to relate to.

Actually, I'm with Ricky: I believe in God as 'this incredibly benevolent force' in the universe, a God who is intimate, intense and immanent – ingrained in the very substance of the world. God, for me, is a radical presence in everything, which is best understood not as an entity over there – an object among other objects – but as the mystery at the core of ordinary reality.

God is everywhere and in everything; or, to be more precise, everything is in God. So we don't need to ask God to draw near, or to be present in our lives. God is already there! We don't need to look for God in some special place: a church, a mosque or a synagogue. God is radically present with us, closer even than our breath. Indeed, the word 'spirit' actually means 'breath'. God's Spirit is the breath of creation, the breath in our lungs, the Spirit of the cosmos, the life force within every human being and every creature on earth. The book of Job, for example, says that if God 'decided to hold his breath, every man, woman, and child would die for lack of air'.*

There is also a lovely comment in the *Gospel of Thomas* where Christ says, 'I am the light above everything. I am in everything. Everything came forth from me, and everything reached me. Split wood, I am there. Lift up a rock, you will find me there.'†

A bad Christian is someone who becomes aware of the

---

* Job 34:14–15 (*The Message* translation).
† The *Gospel of Thomas* is one of many early Christian writings that wasn't included in the final compilation of the Bible. Unlike the New Testament Gospels it has no narrative account of Christ's life but consists entirely of his sayings, many of which also appear in the New Testament Gospels. It's well worth reading alongside the other Gospels.

divine presence in the world and who learns to cultivate that awareness.

I was at a Moby concert recently (the New York music producer, DJ and photographer). I went expecting to enjoy some music, to hear some new songs and see a musician I admire. But it turned out to be a spiritual experience where I bumped into God – as well as bumping (literally) into three thousand people crammed into the Roundhouse in Camden. Leaving that place, I felt I had been to a 'church' where spirits had been uplifted and life celebrated. People left with smiling souls.

In a book with the wonderful title *Mystical Passion: Spirituality for a Bored Society*, William McNamara says that it's better to stay home and smell a flower, bake an apple pie or sweep a floor than have a spooky, spurious experience at a prayer meeting. It's better to simply enjoy the sunshine or a good show than to meddle curiously and conceitedly with the occult. It's better to romp with the dogs in the back garden than engage in haughty spiritual conversation at church, if the dogs help us to be less egotistical and more God-centred.

This is my kind of spirituality. How can we aspire to some holy life if we can't find God in simple things like a glass of beer, a gig at the Roundhouse, a warm bath, a good kiss, a belly laugh, a hug with a friend, or the satis-faction of a job well done?

The Church holds that certain everyday elements – for example water in baptism, the bread and wine in the Eucharist – mysteriously communicate the divine presence to those being baptised or receiving Communion. However, the logic behind the sacraments is that the entire universe is a vast sacramental system: everything in the world has the possibility to mediate the divine. It is literally impossible not to bump into God in the material and human worlds: 'Split wood, I am there. Lift up a rock, you will find me there.'

Enjoy receiving Communion, but celebrate Christ's presence in every meal, every human interaction. 'Break open any loaf, taste any glass of wine, you'll find me there. Look into the eye of friend or stranger alike, you will see me looking back at you.'

3. It's all you need!

how to love your way to heaven

*The purpose of all major religious traditions is
not to construct big temples on the outside, but to
create temples of goodness and compassion inside,
in our hearts.*

– The Dalai Lama

Kay told me she was a bad Christian.

'I believe in God . . . or something . . . you know what
I mean,' she said. 'And I do my best, like everyone else.

But when I see people going to church, I know it's not for me. I'm not like them. My life's kinda messy. I'm happier praying here at home. This is my church.'

At the time, Kay was organising the funeral of Eric, one of her neighbours. Eric was seventy-one and grew up in Glasgow. But that's about all anyone knew about his background. He had no known relatives, but lived in the Holloway area of North London for thirty years, where he was a popular figure, always joking with kids and helping old people – and never seen without his funny tartan hat with its woolly bobble on top. Kay took Eric into her (very extended) family, giving him Sunday dinner every week, along with her children and grand-children, their friends and whoever else happened to be around. 'Come on in – it'll stretch!' was her oft-quoted philosophy.

There's a line in a Nick Cave song that says, 'She's got a house-big heart where we all live.' That's a pretty good description of Kay – a heart as big as a house.

When she realised that, with no next of kin and hardly a penny to his name, Eric would be buried in a common grave without a headstone or any means of identifica-tion, Kay organised a whip-round among her neighbours to pay for the funeral. So Eric was lovingly laid to rest in his own grave, proudly bearing his name. And it was my honour to conduct the service in which Kay gave a simple, moving tribute to her Scottish friend.

However, the full extent of Kay's generosity only became clear a year later when I discovered that, in the event, she had only managed to raise half the money for the funeral, so she had cut a deal with the funeral director to pay the rest over three years out of her own very meagre income. After hearing this, I invited several people in the church to clear the debt, and a couple of days later we were able to hand over the outstanding amount.

As I mentioned in the first chapter, Christians were originally called 'people of the way' – people who followed the example of Jesus in making love a way of life. Using this measure, Kay is easily as good a Christian as anyone I know, and a lot better than most. Believe me, if there is a heaven, Kay is at the front of the queue!

Too often, the gauge used to judge the genuineness of a person's faith is their beliefs: do they believe a, b and c? Do they measure up to what is deemed orthodox faith? But Jesus had a different approach. He was less concerned with a person's beliefs (their orthodoxy) than with their behaviour (their orthopraxis). He said, 'This is how everyone will recognize that you are my disciples – when they see the love you have for each other.'* Love is what matters; the rest is window dressing.

But we don't need to be told this, do we? We instinctively know that love is what counts; that all you need is love. It's in the DNA of every religious tradition, every moral system. Every bad Christian/Jew/Buddhist/Muslim/Hindu/ humanist knows that love is the golden rule: do unto others as you would have them do unto you.

No one in their right mind would suggest that hatred, unkindness or cruelty were virtues or representative of what religion is really about. Sure, there are crackpots in every community who go about hurting and killing in the name of their 'god', but the rest of us know that this is rubbish and nothing to do with religion. St Paul hits the nail on the head when he says that even if we have faith enough to move mountains, we are nothing without love.

Paul also argues that love is the fulfilment of the law. In other words, every religious rule and precept is really just an attempt to legislate what love looks like in practice. At best, laws are sorry substitutes for the real deal, which is love.

However, as we all know, theory is one thing, practice another. Sometimes love is really hard work; on occasions

---

* See John 13:35 (*The Message*)

it's seemingly impossible. So it helps to remind ourselves that love isn't primarily an emotion, but a choice, an act of the will, a decision to work for the well-being of the other person, even when it means sacrificing our own well-being. Love is not about pink fluffy feelings. It isn't even necessarily dependent on liking the other person.

Jesus told his listeners that there are only two laws that matter. If these are followed, the rest can be forgotten. The first is to love God with all your heart, soul and mind, and the second is to love your neighbour as yourself.

But what does it mean to love God? How are we supposed to do this? By singing hymns, doing religious things, saying lots of prayers? Not necessarily. There are even places in the Bible where it says that God detested such things – when the so-called 'worshippers' were, at the same time, oppressing the poor, fiddling their finances and perpetrating injustice.

Loving God isn't necessarily a religious activity. You don't need to be a Christian, Jew or Muslim to love God. You don't need to attend a church or mosque, or follow some kind of ritual. Loving God is much more basic than this, much more routine and human. There are actually millions of ways to love God, most of which have nothing to do with church and religion. For example, we love God when:

we relish our many human gifts and live life with gratitude;
we fill our lungs with fresh air and feel glad to be alive;
we enjoy, and care for, God's creation;
we live fully in the present moment, perhaps appreciating
    details of life we mostly take for granted;
we forgive a wrong done against us;
we take action to make the world a fairer place;
we eat, and drink, and enjoy shelter with thankful hearts
    – offering a prayer for those less fortunate.

However, it's impossible to separate the two command-ments: we cannot love God without loving our neighbour. This is the point that Jesus makes in the parable of the Good Samaritan. Two religious leaders ignored the injured man who had been robbed and was left half-dead at the side of the road. Scurrying off to fulfil their reli-gious duties, they passed by on the other side. But a Samaritan, despised by many Jews at the time and thought to be unclean before God, came to the wounded man's assistance, even paying for his care and recovery.

Who cares if the Samaritan didn't fulfil all the 'right' religious duties – the injured man certainly didn't care! Who's bothered that Kay doesn't attend church regularly – a woman who constantly puts herself out to be kind and loving to people? Isn't this what counts?

But wait. There's a further element to the command-ment that Jesus quotes, which says, 'You shall love your neighbour as yourself.' The assumption, often over-looked, is that we do indeed love our own selves. But do we? And what does it mean to love our selves?

Self-love, in this context, is not the same as narcissism or selfish egotism; it's about self-respect, self-acceptance. It means to value oneself. We might imagine that the Church would be a great place to develop self-esteem. Isn't the gospel all about God loving every single individual, uniquely? Yet in practice many people find their self-esteem undermined in church by guilt at not matching up to certain expectations, or because of a preoccupation with sin and punitive images of God.

When I worked as a chaplain in a hospital treating people with HIV/AIDS, I met Brian, an elegant gay man in his early fifties. He was about to go home for the week-end, but asked if he could meet me first. Brian was troubled by a recurring sense that God hated him for being gay. He grew up a Catholic. And, despite having adopted a gay lifestyle, and having lived with a partner whom he adored for twenty years, Brian never managed to dump the belief instilled in him as a teenager that homosexuality was a mortal sin.

Now, faced with the prospect of meeting his Maker

sooner rather than later, the feeling that God rejected him tormented Brian. I reassured him that he was a beautiful human being; that God was proud of him, just as his friends and family were proud of him. I said that the only thing I could think of that God would hate was Brian's guilt at loving his beloved Michael as he did.

It was an uphill battle. We agreed to chat further after the weekend, but Brian never returned. He took his life. I was devastated. And furious that such misery was inflicted in the name of a loving God. My only consolation is my deep belief that Brian is now finding out what it is to be truly and fully loved by God.

Self-esteem flourishes in a context of approval and acceptance. How different Brian's life might have been had he known such a context in the Church (it's incidental that he was a Catholic; he could well have had a similar experience in other parts of the Church, including the Church of England). At his funeral, his distraught mother railed against the religion that had tormented her son. 'Why did you do this to a man whose heart was filled with love?' she cried. 'Why did you crucify my beautiful son?' The irony in her words seeped into my soul as I heard the voice of God calling from the heart of a grieving mother.

Within Christianity, the sense of unconditional love begins at the baptism of a child, which should be understood not as a reminder of the (mistaken) notion of original sin, but as a symbol of divine grace, of unqualified acceptance. In a consumerist, celebrity-obsessed culture, what could be better than to assert the priceless value of a tiny scrap of humanity: a child who has achieved nothing other than surviving their entry into the world, and contributed nothing apart from the gift of their presence?

But it doesn't stop there. We all need to know God's love as a practical reality. Sadly, this didn't happen for Brian – not in this world, anyway. And it was seeing what condemnation and exclusion did to him that fired my passion and vision for inclusive churches, where God's unconditional love is communicated and where difference is embraced and celebrated. There is nothing more fundamental to the Christian faith than the message that God loves us, come what may. It's what the word 'grace' means: God's gratuitous acceptance. Whenever conditions are attached to God's love, the gospel is undermined and falsified.

Sadly, in my all-too-brief encounter with Brian, I failed to communicate God's grace sufficiently to stop him taking his own life. But I have seen many, many lives transformed by the realisation of God's unqualified love. This, I think, is the real power of the Christian message, so often buried under tons of religious dogma that has nothing to do with the teaching of Christ.

Knowing that God loves and values us can enable us to value ourselves better, to develop self-respect. And this provides the basis for making better choices in life, for strengthening personal integrity, and for empowering us to decide who and what we wish to be, instead of being pushed around by the whims of others or by the fashions and fads of the wider culture.

When I look at our young people at St Luke's, many of whom I baptised, who are now leaving for college or university or starting jobs, I feel thrilled that they are entering the big wide world with high levels of self-respect rooted in the knowledge of God's love, which they have experienced in this community as well as in their families.

The heart and soul of all true religion is this: to love and be loved. The Bible only gives one definition of God: God is love. And in what must be one of the most inclusive statements in Scripture, St John writes, 'Those who live in love live in God, and God lives in them.'*

Greg is a local parishioner who also organised a funeral for someone with no next of kin: a seventy-five-year-old

---

* 1 John 4:16 *Common Worship: Pastoral Services* (Church House Publishing, 2000).

called George. Greg is the caretaker of the block of flats where George lived – and what a caretaker he turned out to be! Going far beyond the call of duty, he came to the crematorium, bringing with him his wife, his small child in a pushchair and his mother-in-law. This little foursome constituted the entire congregation, present to bid George farewell from this world. Just before I dispatched the coffin through the curtains, Greg approached it, stood for a few moments in silence, and then said a touching good-bye to George, planting a kiss on the plain wooden box. Holding back my tears, I silently pondered how wonderful it was that George's passing was not alone; that a civic duty was transcended by friendship and tender love.

Greg is a rough-and-ready North Londoner who makes no claim to faith. I don't expect to see him in church, apart from when his wife drags him along to the odd Christmas service. But if those who practise love live in God and God lives in them, then, like Kay, Greg is loving his way to heaven. No question!

None of us loves all of the time. It can be hard to remain loving towards our nearest and dearest, let alone towards our enemies or those we find stroppy and uncooperative. And it can be hardest of all to love our own selves.

But this is how it is. We are imperfect human beings.

We are works in progress. Guilt and fear cannot make us love; we learn to love only by allowing ourselves to be loved.

God accepts you.

Can you?

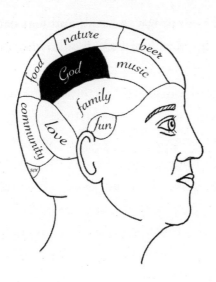

4. It's not about the rules

how to think with your soul

People today are not looking for doctrine or dogma
– we are searching for meaning.

— Michael Meegan

While twiddling my thumbs waiting for a bride to arrive for her wedding at St Luke's, I chatted with Paul, a singer who had been hired by the happy couple to give what turned out to be a sensational performance of the Luther Vandross song 'Always and Forever'.

When he entered the church, Paul immediately fell in love with the wonderful deep-blue painting hanging behind the font. After looking at this, he proceeded to journey, admiringly, around all the artwork in the church. We ended up having a fascinating and wide-ranging conversation about art, the Church, theology and God – all before the bride arrived!

It turned out that Paul had grown up going to church, but had left it all behind five years earlier. However, it wasn't God he left behind; in fact, he said he actually felt closer to God and more spiritually alive after he stopped going to church. And he was pleasantly surprised to hear me say that I could understand this. 'I wish I'd met you ten years ago!' he replied.

Paul felt that the Church still treated him like a child even after he had grown up. 'It was as if I never graduated from Sunday school,' he said. 'I was expected to take everything they told me as gospel, without question. Which was OK when I was a kid, but when I was twenty . . . twenty-five . . . thirty . . .'

For Paul, church was all about conforming. So when he got fed up with conforming, he left. But he didn't leave his faith behind. Far from it; that simply evolved into a different shape.

I enjoyed Paul's vivacious personality, his warm spirit

and easy spirituality – not to mention his silky-smooth singing voice! Even as we talked, I mourned afresh that churches so often frustrate, alienate and ultimately lose some of their best souls. It seems ironic and devastating that an organisation whose *raison d'être* is to help people grow and mature spiritually sometimes ends up hampering that process – or simply being left behind as an irrelevancy.

Some of the most spiritually perceptive people I know are not regular churchgoers. Many, like Paul, have given up going; others never went in the first place. By the same token, there are dyed-in-the-wool churchgoers whose spirituality is, frankly, stunted and infantile. Someone recently said to me, 'I don't go to church because it feels like returning to the spiritual nursery.' Harsh words! But it's a sentiment many share.

The fact is, going to church is not the same as being spiritual; and bailing out of church does not automatically equate with abandoning faith or spirituality. Even as I write, I have just received an e-mail from a woman in Sydney who states, 'I've disconnected from religion to stay connected to God.'

Now yes, of course there are plenty of churchgoers with wonderfully developed spirituality, just as there are church communities where an open and critical approach to faith is encouraged. But sadly, religion and spirituality do not always go together. And we need to understand why.

Neurological research may offer a clue, with the discovery of another form of intelligence, identified as 'spiritual intelligence': a capacity shown to be hardwired into our brains – linked in part to a mass of neural tissue located in the brain's temporal lobes known as the 'God Spot'. This is a neural mass dedicated to making us ask fundamental questions of meaning about existence and to making us search for fundamental answers. Spiritual intelligence has no necessary connection with religion and operates quite independently of religious beliefs, though it has a massive bearing on how we interpret our beliefs.

Of course we all know about logical intelligence (IQ), our capacity to process and apply knowledge in a rational fashion. For a long time, this was the only sort of intelligence that was recognised as important or valid. But by the mid-1980s multiple intelligences were acknowledged, affirming that, while a person may not have great linguistic intelligence, for example, they may possess enormous musical or physical intelligence.

Later, in the 1990s, Daniel Goleman changed the whole intelligence paradigm by popularising neurological research that showed that emotional intelligence (EQ) is of equal importance to logical intelligence. EQ provides awareness of other people's feelings, as well as our own. It enables empathy, compassion and the capacity to respond to other people's pain or pleasure. It enables us to 'read' people and situations at an emotional level. And, unlike IQ, which is generally thought to remain fairly static throughout our lives, EQ can be cultivated and improved: there are ways to develop our emotional intelligence.

Then, towards the end of the 1990s, neurological research suggested that the brain possessed a third basic intelligence, which gives access to deep meaning, fundamental values and an abiding sense of purpose to our lives. Danah Zohar and Ian Marshall, leading experts in this field, identified this intelligence as SQ, spiritual intelligence.

SQ drives us to explore the big questions: Why am I here? What is the purpose of life? Which path should I follow? Why is there something rather than nothing? Spiritual intelligence is all about the big picture; it looks for an overarching sense of meaning to life. SQ is also a capacity that can be cultivated and nurtured. We can improve and grow our spiritual intelligence.

To repeat, SQ has no necessary connection with

religion. Some people channel their spiritual intelligence through a religious tradition, others don't. Atheists and humanists may have a very high SQ, while vociferous 'believers' may have a very low SQ. Spiritual intelligence is rooted in structures of the brain that give the ability to form beliefs in the first place – along with meanings, values and purpose. In that sense, it is more fundamental than religion. As a Christian, I would say it is part of how we are created in the divine image.

Spiritual intelligence is thinking with the soul. Paul's questioning, which so unsettled the people in his church, was not just at an intellectual level: it came from his soul. He longed for deeper meaning and deeper answers, and this led him to deconstruct his faith – not in a negative way, or for negative reasons, but as part of his inner journey. When we talked, it was clear that he still held many of his original beliefs, but he held them in a different way. He had needed to reconstruct them within a different, larger framework.

Quite legitimately, churches are places where beliefs are taught and affirmed, but they must also be places where spiritual intelligence is nurtured. This means creating the space where beliefs can be questioned and doubted and explored – in an open fashion. There is no problem with reciting creeds as classic symbols of faith, provided we can also interrogate them, argue with them and debate about them – and perhaps write some new ones that grapple with the meaning of faith in the twenty-first century, rather than the fourth!

Paul's church had a dogged commitment to certain Christian beliefs, but precious little developed spiritual intelligence with which to process and interpret those beliefs. This became a deal-breaker for Paul, who just got fed up and moved on.

Paul is a classic 'bad Christian': someone with a fairly well-developed SQ, but a low threshold of tolerance for religious crap; someone with an effective moral compass, but impatient with rigid moral codes.

According to Danah Zohar, both IQ and EQ essentially play within the boundaries, but SQ has a propensity to play *with* the boundaries. In other words, it is the intelligence that prompts us to criticise or question the status quo, allowing us to imagine situations and possibilities that do not yet exist – which is surely what real faith is supposed to be like!

So what is it like to think with the soul? What does spiritual intelligence look like in practice? Its qualities include:

self-awareness – having an understanding of what makes us tick, in terms of values and motivations;

principle – staying true to our deepest convictions and values, even if it means standing against the crowd;

spontaneity – living in the moment and responding to what each moment presents;

empathy – the ability to identify with others and share in their feelings;

humility – having a measured sense of our place in the wider scheme of things;

curiosity – the motivation to explore, especially the 'why?' questions;

flexibility – the ability to stand back from a situation or problem and see the bigger picture, and make necessary readjustments;

resilience – remaining positive in the face of adversity, and able to learn and grow from mistakes and setbacks;

being centred or grounded – having a sense of bearing and purpose;

receptivity – staying open and welcoming towards diversity and difference.

Cultivating such qualities requires, first, a commitment to the inner journey – a willingness to penetrate our own façades and pretences to discover more fully who we are and who we want to be. This can be joyful and challenging as we uncover our strengths and vulnerabilities, our potentialities and brokenness, our higher aspirations and deeper motivations. Greater self-awareness is fundamental to the spiritual journey. For me, the Enneagram – a system of understanding different types of personality – is an invaluable tool for self-understanding, and contributes massively to my own quest for increased spiritual intelligence. More on this below.

A second key to fostering SQ is the development of spiritual practices. A spiritual practice is just a device to help you to be more open and attentive:

to yourself – what you are feeling but trying to ignore; what thoughts you are shoving to the back of your mind but ought to listen to; what your body is telling you when you just keep pushing it;

to other people – loved ones whose concerns or joys you tend to overlook; strangers who become invisible but may require your attention;

to situations – circumstances in your life that may be saying important things to you or about you;

to the world in general – little things or great things, things of beauty, details that you forget to notice and be enriched by;

to God – who is present in all these other ways, seeking to guide and enrich you.

A list of suggested practices can be found in Appendix 1, but includes, for example, the Quaker practice of regularly spending time in silence, perhaps just being aware of your breathing; centring prayer, or using a simple repetitive prayer in order to become more grounded in the peace of God's Spirit; a daily walk-and-talk with God.

Third, we cultivate spiritual intelligence within communities of kindred spirits. Sometimes, like Paul, we have to get out of a church in order to grow – or simply to retain our sanity! But ultimately we need to journey with other people: with friends who will affirm us but also speak truthfully to us, and with a wider group where we find stimulation and empowerment.

This sense of spiritual fraternity may be found in an informal but regular gathering of friends, perhaps over a meal, or in a group like Holy Joes, designed to provide space for meaningful interaction – or even in a regular church.

No church is perfect, but there are many around that do allow room for people to question and doubt and discover their own way. Lucia is a good example of someone who returned to church after some years of being away, and discovered a community where her spiritual life flourished:

It wouldn't be an exaggeration to say that re-engaging with a Christian community like St Luke's has shaken my life to its core. I've learned what it feels like to be part of a group of people with God's love at its centre, where I can share and explore my faith with others – but one that, crucially, respects and values every member. I arrived as someone who felt they'd made a lot of mistakes in their life, but it taught me to let go of all that and live, instead, in the present. Not to ignore the things that my conscience was telling me, or allow myself the luxury of ignoring the things that were making me suffer, but ultimately to be embraced as part of who I am. I learned how to read the Bible – not as a 'rule book' for how to live one's life, but as a place, among many others, to go to in search of snapshots of God's wisdom, Jesus' courage, humility and love. One night, sharing a meal with other people who were there like me, to talk about their experiences of faith, I understood the sharing of the Communion bread in a whole new light. It was about friendship, warmth, inclusion.

Religion and spiritual intelligence should go together, but too often they don't. Spiritual intelligence allows people to be creative, to explore new possibilities, to change the rules and alter situations, while religion is frequently associated with a rigid status quo, with formality, narrow-mindedness and traditionalism.

However, the gulf between the two need not exist, as Jesus himself demonstrated. He was a truly faithful Jew, but he interpreted and practised his Judaism with massive spiritual intelligence. This constantly landed him in the bad books of a rigid, unspiritual religious establishment: when he focused on the spirit of the law instead of on literal obedience; when he placed the needs of people ahead of rules; when he ignored conventional boundaries for the sake of love; when he challenged unthinking conformity and freed people from false guilt.

I am a bad Christian. I often struggle with church subculture and sometimes find myself more at home among honest 'pagans'. But I have never erred in my passionate love of the figure of Jesus. He, more than anyone else, embodies the spiritual energy and intelligence that I admire and covet so much.

Jesus said, 'Truly I tell you, whoever does not receive the kingdom of God as a little child will never enter it.'* Spiritual intelligence is not being clever enough to answer hard questions; it's being open enough to see life and others afresh through the eyes of a child. It requires that

---

* Mark 10:15.

we cease taking refuge in what we think we know to constantly explore and learn from what we don't know. It requires that we give up the addiction to certainty and learn to appreciate the virtue of questions. With great spiritual intelligence, the poet Rainer Maria Rilke advises us to embrace and learn to love life's difficult questions, treating them like locked rooms that we can't enter, or like books written in a language we can't understand. Don't go chasing answers that aren't available to you now, he says, but rather, 'Live the questions now.'* Then gradually we may learn to live our way into the answers. And this, surely, is what matters: to live our way into the answers to life's great dilemmas, rather than simply trying to possess the answers like trophies to our great intellect.

---

* Quoted from Danah Zohar and Ian Marshall, *Connecting with our Spiritual Intelligence* (Bloomsbury, 2000).

5. Wakey! Wakey!

how to make sure you live before you die

I don't want to end up simply having visited this world.

– Mary Oliver

It was one of the most dramatic conversion experiences I have seen – a complete transformation. Yet it had nothing to do with church or religion. Jesus didn't even get a mention!

It took place in the upstairs room of a pub where I was

leading an Enneagram workshop.* Only a couple of people in the group knew I was a priest. Very few of those present had any religious connections that I knew about.

The workshop was spread over two consecutive weekends. We began with everyone introducing themselves. Slicing through the niceties of the occasion, Susan, an attractive and enthusiastic woman, shockingly announced, 'When I enter a room full of people, the first thing I do is look around and decide which men I'd be prepared to go to bed with.'

Well, that definitely got everyone's attention!

The woman sitting next to me muttered, 'Bloody hussy.'

Most of the men in the room looked sheepish, probably wondering if they had a chance.

Over the course of the two weekends, people engaged in searching self-reflection, linked to their particular personality type. Some took their time getting into the process, others moved faster. Susan threw herself into it headlong.

At the end of the second weekend, there was feedback on what everyone had learned. Susan broke down and

---

* The Enneagram is a powerful system for identifying different types of personality, and understanding why we do the things we do. For more information about the Enneagram, go to www.dave-tomlinson.co.uk.

said that this had been the most challenging experience of her life. 'The impression I gave in the first session was probably misleading,' she said. 'It's true, I have slept with a lot of men in my time. But, you know, I never really fancied any of them. Actually, I could hardly bear most of them kissing me. What I really wanted was intimacy. But there was precious little of that! After each time I was just left feeling empty and lonely and disgusted . . . mostly with myself.'

Through smudged eyeliner she spoke of now going home to a different life. 'I really want to start respecting myself,' she said. 'Maybe even learning to like myself a bit. The only way I can describe what's happened over this past week is that I've woken up. It's like I've been sleepwalking through life. And now, all of a sudden, I'm wide awake . . . like I've been born again . . . if that doesn't sound too weird.'

The workshop was non-religious, yet it was deeply religious. There was no talk of God or Christ, yet the Holy Spirit permeated everything. A very real conversion took place before our eyes, as Susan awoke to a new realisation of who she was and who she could be. We witnessed a new birth.

There wasn't a dry eye in the house!

Sleepwalking on the inside is something we all do,

when life seems boring, or painful, or too demanding, or when we don't like the person we're with, or when we're anxious and worried, or just wish we were somewhere else. We switch off, disappear on the inside, perhaps numb out in front of a TV or computer screen, have a drink, fantasise about the future, romanticise the past – and fall asleep to the present moment.

Yet that's what life is – moments. And as Susan's story shows, it's possible to sleep through an awful lot of moments, years and years of them. Which is why we need periodic wake-up calls that say, 'This is your life! Wake up! Stop sleeping through it!'

Maybe a health scare sounds the alarm, an accident, a near miss, the death of a loved one, a financial crisis or some other random jolt of circumstance. It may even be through a deliberate process of self-reflection, like Susan's.

The essential thing is to wake up – to make sure that we get to live before we die!

Jesus was all about this – waking people up. 'I came that they may have life, and have it abundantly,' he said.*
Which is another way to say, 'I came to wake people up, to save them from the stupor of mere existence.'

---

* John 10:10.

Throughout his ministry, Jesus constantly snapped his fingers in front of people, rousing them from slumber and alerting them to new possibilities for themselves, for the wider community, for the world. With a new vision of reality that he called the kingdom of God, he demonstrated that things don't have to be the way they are; that a different path is available to those prepared to wake up to it.

The heart of Christ's message was the love of God. He brought to ordinary people – downtrodden by ruthless rulers – the sense of their belovedness. Each person Jesus touched knew, perhaps for the first time, that their life mattered; that they were loved and cherished. In all her soul-destroying liaisons, this is what Susan was searching for – it's what we all crave – but she was looking in the wrong places.

To know our belovedness changes everything. From this foundation we can learn to respect and value our lives, to value each moment, each experience, whether joyful or challenging, because all of our existence matters and merits being lived, and not slept through.

The American writer and theologian Frederick Buechner expresses this magnificently when he says, 'Listen to your life. See it for the fathomless mystery that it is. In the boredom and pain of it, no less than in the excitement and gladness: touch, taste, smell your way to the holy and hidden heart of it, because in the last analysis all moments are key moments, and life itself is grace.'*

What Buechner describes is a state of wakefulness: of realising that our life is precious in all its details, even the painful and difficult bits. Every moment is a key moment. When we live like this, in the moment, we are coming close to the kingdom of God.

When Jesus proclaimed the kingdom of God, he wasn't promoting a religious institution or a theological theory; he was talking about a condition – a state of being awake to God and to all the possibilities that being awake to God opens up. The kingdom of God is a state of profound wakefulness, and to become wholly awake, or to experience even a drop of life fully, is to open oneself to the kingdom of God. We might say, giving a twist to the words of St John, that 'God is eternal wakefulness, and those who live in wakefulness live in God and God lives in them'.

To be wakeful means to be open and receptive to all that life offers. In order to achieve this, Jesus says that we must become as little children who, in their wide-eyed wonder, demonstrate perfectly what it is to welcome the

---

* Frederick Buechner, *Now and Then: A Memoir of Vocation*, (HarperSanFrancisco, 1991).

world with joyful abandon. A child does not try to anticipate the future, or become anxious about what may be; a
child is right there, in the moment, alive, now – receptive
to the circumstance, to the person, to the possibility. To
experience this childlike openness is to experience the
kingdom of heaven, Jesus says.

But the hurts and disappointments of life often cause
us to shut down, to batten down the hatches against
further pain or sadness, to become cautious and suspicious, less receptive. And something within us contracts.
Our spiritual energy diminishes. Any sense of mystery or
wonder shrinks. We may feel safer, perhaps. But we die a
little in the process. And we become spiritually slothful –
sleepy to the adventure that is life.

When life brings a hardship – a broken relationship, an
illness, redundancy, a disappointment, a long queue – the
temptation is to fall asleep, to become slothful on the
inside, to blank out the hardship and stop living. But life is
there to be lived: the abundant life that Jesus promised.

My friend Nick knew he was dying of cancer. But
instead of moping around in a dosed state, waiting to
depart, he decided to live. He set up a website called
'Laughing with Cancer'* to say that the disease that

---

* www.laughingwithcancer.com – be sure to check out the blog.

wreaks havoc in so many lives can also contain a hidden gift that may give meaning and purpose to those lives.

Nick died on 26 October 2010, but as Julia says in her blog on the website, Nick never expected Laughing with Cancer to cure his illness. The purpose of creating the site was to be as alive and as present as possible for whatever time he had, with or without a cure. And it worked. Nick never lost the scent for living; he never glazed over on the inside.

Wakefulness is what the Buddhists call mindfulness, a state of being alert to even the smallest and most ordinary details of life. Jesus gives a delightful insight into divine wakefulness or mindfulness when he says that even a sparrow does not fall to the ground without God noticing. This is a powerful reminder of God's attentiveness to the details of our lives too: 'even the hairs of your head are all counted. So do not be afraid.'*

The Christian approach to mindfulness is encapsulated in the practice of gratitude. 'Give thanks to God the Father at all times and for everything,'† St Paul says. Martin Luther King Jr described gratitude as the basic Christian attitude. In other words, whoever experiences thankfulness is practising the core value of Christianity.

---

* Matthew 10:30.
† Ephesians 5:20

The thirteenth-century mystic and theologian Meister Eckhart said that if the only prayer you ever say in your entire life is 'thank you', it will be enough.

There are two ways to be thankful. The first is thankfulness as a spontaneous emotion. This is what happens either when something good comes your way and you feel overwhelmed with gratitude, or on those unconstrained occasions when you just sense an upsurge of thankfulness for life itself. I'll give you an example.

On a crisp but beautifully bright day in early spring, my wife Pat and I sat on a bench outside the cottage that we rent as a getaway in Yorkshire. The house sits alone in a deserted valley with no electricity, no satellite dish, no WiFi. Gazing at the peaceful scenery, a cup of coffee in hand, listening to the call of two buzzards echoing across the valley, I felt a great swell of gratitude.

Then it happened. About three metres in front of us, a little animal walked along the drystone wall. It was a weasel – presumably a female, as it was carrying a tiny wriggling baby weasel in its mouth. After a few moments the animal ran back along the wall without the kit. And then, to our delight, she appeared again with another of her brood. Over a period of fifteen minutes we watched this wonderful little creature transport her entire litter, presumably to a safer nest site.

Watching the care, patience and energy of the whole event made me think about the words of Jesus: 'Jerusalem . . . how often have I desired to gather your children together as a hen gathers her brood under her wings.'* He might well have said, 'How often I desired to gather your children as a mother weasel gathers her kits into a warm, safe nest.' And I felt thankful, privileged and very much more alive for having been present that day – the day the weasels moved house.

The second way to be thankful is thankfulness as a practice. A practice is a way of living or being, born from habit. It's not spontaneous, but deliberate and persistent; something we decide to cultivate. In time, the habit builds into a practice that shapes our life and character. Grateful people are mindful people, awake to the mystery of existence, attentive to others, alive in the moment.

The dining table in our vicarage has seen some extraordinarily happy times. I can think of no greater pleasure than eating, drinking, laughing and telling stories with lovely guests – and we have lots of very lovely guests. But often, when we're just at home with our daughter Jeni, her husband Paul and our grandson Jude, eating an ordinary evening meal in the kitchen,

---

* Matthew 23:37.

Jeni will suddenly announce, 'You know what? It don't get better than this!' We all grin, and sometimes say a hearty 'Amen, sister!' It's a simple and humorous yet profound practice, which helps us all stay alive to the wonder of ordinary life in the vicarage.

The Christian celebration of the Eucharist quintessentially expresses grateful awareness – the very word 'Eucharist' means thankfulness or gratitude. So the central ritual in Christianity is a feast of gratitude.

On the face of things, it may seem absurd to talk of a 'feast'. What kind of feast boasts a pinch of bread and a sip of wine? But that's the whole point. In a world where entire meals are consumed in forgetfulness, there's something powerful and evocative about focusing attention, gratefully, on one tiny morsel. Many in the world are hungry. When I receive Communion I know I am fortunate, and I feel compassion for all those who have no bread and no friends or family. For this alone, regular participation in the Eucharist serves as an important practice of grateful awareness.

However, for Christians, the Eucharist speaks of much more. It's a celebration of divine generosity in which we feast afresh on the love that welcomes all, unconditionally and without exception. When I invite people to receive Communion I declare this to be the table of Christ, where all are welcome and no one is turned away. So we affirm God's unrestricted acceptance by offering bread and wine to everyone present without question or condition.

But the Eucharist also reminds us that love comes at a price. The focal point of Christian worship centres on the brutal execution of an innocent victim, who demonstrates even in death the redemptive power of love. There is no pain avoidance in the eucharistic celebration, no dodging of the world's darkness, or denial of human ugliness. There is a genuine acknowledgement that life can be rubbish. But ultimately, love, mercy and beauty triumph.

I love the story of Victor Frankl, the Jewish psychotherapist who was imprisoned by the Nazis in a concentration camp and survived to write about his experiences. He tells of an afternoon in one of the camps when the men had tramped back several miles from their work site and were lying exhausted, sick and hungry in their barracks. It was in the winter, and they had marched through a cold, dispiriting rain. Suddenly one of the men burst into the barracks and shouted for the others to come outside. Reluctantly, but sensing the urgency in the man's voice, they stirred themselves and staggered into the courtyard. The rain had stopped, and a bit of sunlight was breaking through under the lumpy, leaden clouds. It was reflecting on the little pools of water standing about on the concrete floor of the courtyard. 'We stood there,' said Frankl, 'marvelling at the goodness of the creation. We were tired and cold and sick, we were starving to death, we had lost our loved ones and never expected to see them again, yet there we stood, feeling a sense of reverence as old and formidable as the world itself!'

Each day, each moment, we face the choice between life and death. Victor Frankl and his companions chose life, despite being surrounded by the stench of death. Instead of sleepwalking through a devastatingly ugly situation, they found within it a source of joy and beauty that kept their spirits alive.

Henry David Thoreau once said, 'I wanted to live deep and suck out all the marrow of life . . . and not, when I came to die, discover I had not lived.'

Life or death? The choice is yours.

6. Dumping the guilt trip

how to forgive yourself and move on

It is not what you are or what you have been that
God looks at with his merciful eyes, but what you
desire to be.

– from *The Cloud of Unknowing*

It was the January sale at the HMV music store in central
London, and I was standing in a long line, waiting to pay
for a handful of CDs I had picked out. I should have been
home ages ago. But the tedious clergy gathering I had

attended that afternoon went on a bit. And then the record store mysteriously sucked me in.

Fidgeting with my phone, texting Pat to say I would be late, I was approached by a security man who ominously asked if he could have a word. I stepped out of the queue. Then, awkwardly, he said, 'Excuse me, Father.' (Oops – I was still wearing a dog collar.) 'I'm sorry, I know you're shopping, but I've been wanting to talk to a priest for a while . . . and then I saw you standing there. I'm not really very religious, but . . . I wonder if you'd mind?'

For the next fifteen minutes Frank told me about something he had done several years before, which had had serious consequences for another person and left him with a mountain of guilt. It was a strange confessional – surrounded by the bustling crowd of HMV shoppers – but right there in the middle of the store, I took Frank's hands, looked him square in the eye and said, 'Frank, God forgives you. Forgive yourself. Go in peace.' He was a big guy. But he cried as I spoke. Then after a short pause, a great smile spread over his face.

We never met again.

Frank had messed up. He knew this. And during our conversation I told him what he also already knew: that he needed to find the person he had injured and try to make amends.

By not dealing with the situation, he allowed the guilty feeling to become an accusing voice in his head, which constantly told him he was a bad person. But he wasn't a bad person. He had done something wrong which he needed to address, but this did not make him a bad person.

I hope our brief encounter enabled Frank to trade in his guilty feelings for the determination to sort out (or at least attempt to sort out) the damage he had caused, and then to move on.

Everyone feels guilty sometimes. Whatever our moral standards, we all fail to live up to them – perhaps most of the time. So we experience guilt. In itself, this is not a bad thing. Guilt is the sting of conscience, the twinge that catches our attention and tells us something is not right. Without it our personal lives and relationships – and society in general – would sink into chaos. The psychopath feels no guilt or remorse, has no apparent moral compass. But the rest of us wrestle with our consciences and with periodic guilt, as we negotiate our way through life's moral dilemmas.

But there's a problem with this, a bug in the system, in that conscience is such a variable gauge. Some of us feel guilt very easily; others seem to get away more or less scot-free a lot of the time. Conscience tells different people different things. Why is this?

Part of it is no doubt due to our different personalities and perceptions. But conscience isn't a fixed entity. While there are many theories about how it works, it's clear that the primary development of conscience is in childhood, where numerous voices contribute to its sensitivities – parents, family, schoolteachers, social attitudes, religion and so on. It's like a complicated piece of software that can be programmed in different ways. Part of growing up and discovering our individuality involves questioning these various 'inputs', modifying our conscience – making independent moral judgements.

But this can be challenging, especially where religion is concerned, because religion is perceived by many to contain God's will and word on moral issues, to be obeyed at all costs. This can lead to agonising dilemmas.

Take Brenda, for example, who, six years after her divorce, still struggled to form a new relationship – because she couldn't exorcise the voice from her head that told her she would be committing adultery. Or the twenty-three-year-old man who had grown up in a conservative church, who was tortured with guilt that he masturbated (despite my telling him that 99 per cent of men masturbate and the other 1 per cent are liars). Or the woman severely disabled by multiple sclerosis who admitted, with shame, that due to her suffering she considered ending her life, but feared she would land up in hell as a result.

Such stories anger me. As someone who believes in a loving God, and who advocates religion as a cure for the afflictions of the soul, I am infuriated when so-called 'faith' multiplies people's troubles rather than solving them, or when God is presented as some punitive, mean-minded tyrant. Over the years, I have spent more time working to release people from false guilt induced by religion and from horribly judgemental images of God than anything else.

Jesus' parable of the Prodigal Son is a great antidote to the image of a judgemental God, presenting instead a wonderful picture of a loving parental figure, full of grace and compassion.

It's a story about a young man who is hungry to taste all that life has to offer – and who wants to have it now! So he persuades his father to hand over his share of the family inheritance immediately, and he squanders it on 'riotous living' in a distant country. Finally, when all the money is gone, with his life in tatters, the desperate young man decides to go home and face his father, whose generosity he has abused.

When he arrives back home, naked and hungry, his father, who had longed for his return, sweeps aside his son's well-rehearsed words of contrition, immediately calling for new clothes and a ring for his finger. He then throws a party to celebrate his son's return – no guilt trip, no call for grovelling apologies, no shameful ticking off. The prodigal needed no forgiveness from his father. That was a done deal long ago. He just needed to come home.

I believe that the fundamental message of Christianity – beautifully set forth in this story – is not that we are sinners who have messed up, but that we are loved by God beyond measure and that nothing we do will cause us to forfeit that love. God does not expect perfection of us; there is no need to grovel and beg forgiveness when we fail. Even in our most monumental screw-ups, all that is required is that we journey home to God's cleansing, restoring love.

Many people I meet feel they could never call themselves Christians because they aren't good enough, because they have messed up in some way, or just feel unworthy. But Christianity is not about being good. We all mess up. It's about a God who always welcomes and never condemns.

Isn't this too good to be true? Don't we have to do something – repent or whatever – in order for God to welcome us and forgive us? Absolutely not! With God, love is unconditional; forgiveness is unilateral. Like the prodigal, we are forgiven from the moment we go off the tracks, long before we decide to come home.

Of course, in order to enjoy this radical love of God, we need to see it, realise it, allow it to become a reality by internalising it; otherwise the feeling of guilt continues. But once you believe God's love to be true, accept that you are beloved of God, it will change your life, I promise. You will be able to ditch the guilt, stop being worried about whether you are good enough, and enjoy a new freedom and confidence.

This is where repentance comes in. To repent literally means 'to go beyond the mind that you have' – to enlarge the scope of what you think is possible. I like to think of repentance as a way of waking up: waking to a new reality, waking to the realisation that things don't have to be the way they were. Your life can be different, can be reshaped. But for this to happen, you need to ditch the guilt by discovering God's unconditional love. God does not do guilt; God does forgiveness.

Finally, what does all this look like in practice? How do we get rid of guilty feelings when, like Frank, we know we have messed up?

Here are my tips for dumping guilt.

1. Identify exactly what it is you feel bad about

General feelings of guilt are useless and should not be tolerated. They quickly dent our confidence and under-mine self-worth. It's important to get to grips with our guilt, perhaps with the help of a friend who can help to isolate the cause. Learning to be specific about guilt is the starting point in dumping it.*

2. Accept responsibility for your actions

The key element in the resolution of guilt is the accept-ance of responsibility. Everything else flows from this. It's how we start to feel forgiven. We are not expected to be faultless, but we do need to accept responsibility. Moral perfectionism – no; moral responsibility – yes.

One important way to accept moral responsibility is through confession – admitting, first and foremost to ourselves, that we were in the wrong. The father of the prodigal may not have needed to hear his son's confes-sion, but the prodigal himself needed to hear it: 'I did this! I screwed up!'

However, often it's very helpful to admit our fault in the presence of another. Which is why the confessional

---

* If general feelings of guilt and shame persist, it may be a sign of depression, so it's important to seek help from a doctor or counsellor.

has always been popular in Catholic spirituality. Or why we often make confessions to a friend, or to a therapist. Or even, in a moment of madness, to a random priest in the middle of a record store. Confession is good for the soul. It's how we accept responsibility for our actions and clear the way to move on. Just picture the tears and the big grin on Frank's face, and you'll know what I mean.

Of course, taking responsibility will almost certainly require admitting our fault to the person we have wronged, as well. This needs to be direct and forthright – and without self-justification. Getting the tone right is also essential: making light trivialises the issue; grovelling cheapens the experience.

3. Make amends where appropriate

Sometimes actions speak louder than words. It may be obvious what needs to be done, or it may require some imagination. But it needs to be appropriate and proportionate to the level of hurt or offence caused. Over-the-top restitution can be embarrassing and awkward. Be sure not to dump your guilt onto the other person!

And sometimes, once we have made our peace, the kindest thing is to get out of the person's face – even the best apology does not necessarily bring about reconciliation.

4. Receive God's forgiveness, forgive yourself, then move on

Sometimes the hardest part lies in forgiving ourselves. There may be lots of reasons for this: perhaps we feel embarrassed about our behaviour and how other people still view it; perhaps we are aware of the continuing pain we caused another person; perhaps we feel that we need to be punished further.

Perhaps we are making the mistake of equating forgiving with forgetting or condoning. So we think that forgiving ourselves is a way of excusing what we have done. But this is not true. Refusing to forgive ourselves is really a refusal to live fully, because it's impossible to live wholly in the moment when we are preoccupied with feelings of guilt. It's also a potential threat to our mental, physical and spiritual well-being. Unforgiveness of any sort requires a lot of energy; we are constantly chewed up. This energy deserves to be put to better use, so that our creativity, abilities and relationships are fed – not our negativity.

So many people seem to carry about so much guilt. Which is why, most Sundays in our services at St Luke's, I include some words of absolution – typically, 'For all the ways in which you have failed to live up to even your own best expectations of yourselves: God forgives you. Forgive yourself. Forgive others.'

People perpetually tell me how important these words are to them. But the real message of this chapter is that by opening ourselves to God's love we can internalise words of forgiveness and make them a gift to ourselves every day.

One final point: sometimes we can't resolve a situation of hurt or wrongdoing with another person because they are dead. But it can still be helpful to express our apology to that person, perhaps in the presence of another person. I have led many people to do this over the years – sometimes with remarkable effect.

I recently met with Sara and her family to discuss the funeral of her father. As I sat in her living room with her two sisters and their brother, I sensed that Sara's grief carried some additional burden. With a little prompting, she confessed to a great rift with her dad, which she had not found the time to address before he died. As with many families, the source of the squabble was embarrassingly trivial, but nonetheless real in its effect.

After chatting for ten minutes, and encouraging Sara not to beat herself up about it, I left my seat and knelt in front of her. As with Frank, I took her hands, looked her in the eye and said, 'Sara, God forgives you. I believe your father forgives you. Forgive yourself.' The whole room was in tears, including her brother, who lightened the atmosphere by saying, 'Wow, Dave! You should do this for a living!'

7. Laughing with God

how to get to heaven by having a good time

As a rule, it was the pleasure-haters who became unjust.

– W. H. Auden

I think God hates religion devoid of pleasure!

There's a wonderful old Jewish proverb that says we will have to give account on Judgement Day of every good thing that we refused to enjoy when we might have done so.

It's a fabulous thought: God ticking people off for not

having enough fun . . . killjoys shipped off to 'pleasure purgatory' to learn how to have a good time before being allowed through the Pearly Gates!

So why, I wonder, is religion so often associated with party-pooping? Why are Christians the ones who don't do things – especially fun things? How did it become a virtue to be straight-laced and prudish? And who decided that God doesn't like beer and rude jokes?

You would be amazed how often a hush comes over a room when I walk in wearing a dog collar. Or how many times in the pub after a funeral some poor kid gets a clip round the ear for swearing 'in front of the vicar'. I hate it when this happens (as does the kid!) – when people pussy-foot around me, trying to protect me from the supposed vulgarities of everyday life.

So I sometimes make a deliberate point of using a bit of colourful language, or lighting up a cigar, or telling a dirty joke, or asking for a whisky when someone offers me a cup of tea (well-meaning parishioners have now filled a whole cupboard in my house with bottles of cheap whisky!). The response to such token expressions of my humanity is invariably positive: 'You're not like a vicar, Dave,' people will say. 'You're normal like us!' And this leads to conversations that are much more real and relaxed – and productive.

C. S. Lewis tells a story about a schoolboy who, when

asked what he thought God was like, replied that as far as he could make out God was the sort of person who is always snooping around to see if anyone is enjoying themselves – and then trying to stop them.

If this is indeed how people picture God, it's no wonder they go quiet when someone like me walks into the room. Which is why I go out of my way to shatter the negative stereotypes people have of vicars, Christianity and God, and try to present more positive impressions.

I have always had a liking for the Laughing Buddha, the rotund, happy figure who symbolises the ideals of the good life: health, happiness, prosperity and longevity. And I regret that in contrast God and Jesus are mostly portrayed as rather stern, austere figures. However, this is not the way that lots of Christians experience God.

The fourteenth-century German mystic Meister Eckhart described God as 'voluptuous and delicious' (you can see why Eckhart had problems with the Pope!). No doubt he had in mind the Latin meaning of 'voluptuous', which is 'pleasure, delight, enjoyment'. Eckhart's God wasn't the snooping killjoy Lewis talks about, but some-one who looks around to see if people are having a good time and then encourages it. A voluptuous God delights in creation, giggles with delight when people enjoy being alive, takes pleasure in human joys.

In my view, presenting God as any kind of cosmic party-pooper is nothing short of blasphemy.

In 2007, two Australians launched an exhibition of pictures entitled 'Jesus Laughing'. As global travellers, they noticed that wherever they went pictures and images of Jesus showed him as a miserable, negative figure. But their reading of the Gospels suggested something different. So they decided to initiate a debate on the notion that Jesus was a cheerful, exciting character and not 'the miserable man in a nighty with a plate attached to his head that is so often portrayed in art'.

They invited artists from around the world to create pictures of Jesus, seen through the lens of their own culture, but joyful or laughing. This resulted in a very special collection of paintings with some quite unconventional images of Jesus – dancing, juggling, playing games with children, eating and drinking and laughing, even performing as a stand-up comic.*

The American writer Anne Lamott says that her two best prayers are 'Help me, help me, help me' and 'Thank you, thank you, thank you'. What this suggests to me is that the two parts of life where we tend to experience God are the times of great pleasure and the times of great anguish.

---

* See 'Jesus Laughing' website at www.jesuschrist.uk.com.

Ironically, I suspect it's in the painful times – the 'Help me, help me, help me' experiences – that we are more aware of God. We call out to God in desperation, even when we're not sure that God exists. But in times of pleasure, our focus is understandably elsewhere: we're consumed with enjoyment. However, bidden or unbidden, God is always present where true happiness is felt and shared.

And the way that we sense and respond to the divine presence in pleasurable moments is in our sense of gratitude – the feeling of 'Thank you, thank you, thank you'. The words may hardly even form in our consciousness, but the sensation of gratitude is something we all experience and this, in essence, is prayer. It's what we can call the 'Hurrah!' reaction – 'hurrah' being the less pious cousin of 'hallelujah'.* Every spirited 'Hurrah!' is really a hallelujah – 'God is here!'

Actually, 'hurrah' probably derives from a Norse term meaning 'on to paradise'. Every experience of real delight and happiness is in its own way a taste of paradise, a foretaste of heaven.

But what constitutes real pleasure or delight? The Greek philosopher Epicurus gave this question a lot of

---

* Hallelujah literally means 'praise the Lord'.

thought. Indeed, his entire philosophical system revolves around the pursuit of a happy, tranquil life, with the absence of pain wherever possible.

He taught that pleasure and pain are the measures of what is good or evil.

Yet while his name has been appropriated for all kinds of hedonistic pursuits, Epicurus himself preferred moderation to over-indulgence. He drank water rather than wine and settled happily for a dinner of bread and olives. His recipe for the good life consisted of friendship, freedom, the pleasures of an examined life and enough food and shelter to keep body and soul together. In other words, he understood that having a good time is not really about self-indulgence, but about knowing the meaning of 'enough', and sharing our enoughness with others.

In a conversation at a party, the writer Joseph Heller was asked how it felt to know that the financier across the room probably earned more money the previous day than Heller made from his book *Catch 22* during all the years of its published life. Heller replied, 'I have something he will never have – enough.'

Research has identified three levels of happiness: what they call the Pleasant Life, the Engaged or Good Life, and the Meaningful Life.

The Pleasant Life is based on having as much pleasure

as we can, as many of the positive emotions and instinc-
tual indulgences as possible. It's about finding financial
security, having great holidays and all the latest gadgets.
Of course, there is nothing wrong with these things, but
this happiness fades quickly, so we become addicted to
more and more of the same, constantly running to find
the next pleasure. This leads to the classic state of 'I've
got everything but I'm not happy'. It's what Jesus called
gaining the world but losing one's soul.

The Engaged or Good Life begins to introduce some of
what we feel is missing when life simply revolves around
the pursuit of pleasure. It's when we start to discover our
particular 'gifts of the Spirit' – our signature strengths or
positive traits (i.e. kindness, curiosity, perseverance, attention to detail and so on) – and learn to use them every
day.* We discover a sense of self-worth, and this brings a
sense of authentic identity and a feeling of happiness
anchored in who we really are and what we have to offer.

The Meaningful Life occurs when we learn to tran-
scend our individuality and feel connected to something
greater than ourselves. By applying our gifts and strengths

---

* I find the Enneagram indispensable in identifying people's key
strengths – see Appendix 2. The website Authentic Happiness also
offers a helpful strength survey that will provide a useful list of your
strengths – www.authentichappiness.org.

for the benefit of this greater cause, rather than just for our own benefit, we discover an engaged happiness that transcends our individual fulfilment.

These three levels of happiness are not a line of progress; we can pursue all three – a balance of pleasure, engagement and meaning that results in a truly good and pleasant life.

Speaking as an Epicure – a lover of pleasure – the Pleasant Life constantly beckons. I dislike painful situations and have a voracious appetite for pleasurable experiences. But what I have learned is that it's vital to live all of my life, not just the happy bits. Meaning and true happiness can only be discovered when we embrace the dark sides of our experience as well as the pleasant sides.

This was brought home to me when I first arrived at my present parish, when I was asked to see Richard, a man with advanced motor neurone disease. Against my natural inclination, I agreed to visit him every week. One of my own signature gifts is to bring fun and cheer to people. I had no idea how to do this with Richard, a man who couldn't speak clearly, with whom I struggled to communicate, and whose illness troubled me.

However, after a few weeks I started to understand that our times together were much more for my sake than Richard's. I suspect that all I brought to him at the beginning was a pair of frightened rabbit's eyes. However, *he* gave *me* a glimpse of heaven. Slowly I recognised a twinkle in his eye that said something like, 'I may be in the grip of this disease, but this is not who I am!' I don't think he was in any way happy with his plight, but his spirit refused to be defined by it. For me, visiting Richard was painful (what an absurd thing to say!), but it was profoundly instructive to my soul.

In order to live fully and completely, we must embrace the darker aspects of life, the night-time as well as the day. There is a curious piece of sculpture in Notre Dame Cathedral in Paris. A leering devil is leaning over and embracing an angel, who in turn is holding the devil. Another figure stands over and behind them, looking down at both with a compassionate eye. Perhaps this other figure is God, or our own eye of discrimination, or both – the quiet divine clarity that is able to embrace the opposites and acknowledge the place of both of them in our lives.* We live in a culture that prefers the ease and comfort of either/or thinking to the complexities of para-dox. We want light without darkness, the glories of spring and summer without the demands of autumn and winter. The truth, as the Quaker Parker Palmer points out, is

---

* I owe this observation to Roger Housden in his book *Seven Sins for a Life Worth Living* (Harmony Books, 2005).

that, split off from each other, neither darkness nor light is fit for human habitation. We need the paradox of darkness and light, pleasure and pain.

Conventional Christian wisdom tells us that nobody gets to heaven for having a good time. I disagree. I believe in a 'voluptuous and delicious' God, a God of pleasure and delight, a God who created sweaty bodies and raucous laughter, cheeky humour and kissing lips, hearty food and rich red wine. If God doesn't want us to enjoy life and fall in love with the world, then existence is a sick joke! And heaven truly is a pipe dream.

8. Change what you can

how to dump bad choices and make good ones

> '*It is our choices, Harry, that show us what we truly are, far more than our abilities.*'
>
> – J. K. Rowling

I met Mairi through a friend who felt I might be able to help her. She was sixteen, but looked and behaved more like a twenty-five-year-old: a beautiful, intelligent, highly articulate young woman with great prospects in life. However, beneath her charming and attractive appearance, Mairi was depressed and secretly self-harmed. Britain has the highest self-harm statistics in Europe, and Mairi fell into the category most at risk: young women aged fifteen to nineteen.

As we talked, I became convinced that she needed more expert help than I could offer, so I arranged for her to see Hilary, a psychotherapist in our church community. Mairi was gay but didn't want to accept this, and couldn't talk with her parents about it. When we met, I almost felt she wanted me, as a priest, to tell her that same-sex relationships were wrong. She seemed angry with God for allowing her to be this way. But she agreed to go to counselling.

After almost a year, Mairi decided that she could stop seeing Hilary. She no longer self-harmed and felt confident to pick up her life and move on. During that time, she made some hard choices, but good ones. Shortly after finishing the sessions, she sent me this moving e-mail:

I'm writing to you to thank you for giving me the opportunity to see someone about my problems. It has changed me hugely as a person, and given me new confidence. The kind that enables a person to smile freely, without worrying what any other person will think of them. The kind that means as you walk down the street you hold your head high and look straight ahead as opposed to down at the pavement below your feet.

It has given me faith and belief in myself, something which I was largely lacking previously. I can't really explain how deeply that has affected my life. Maybe an example will help. Before, if I was to walk into a bar and see a woman I really fancied I'd rather have chewed my hand off and eaten it for dinner than approach or even glance in her direction. There was a whole bundle of insecurities that prevented me from doing so. Now, if I'd had a drink or two I might even manage a half-decent conversation!

Thinking back it all seems so surreal. And a bit of a miracle. It's restored my faith in God . . . I don't see any other way it could have all come together without there being some sort of guide. That and the fact that you're a priest. Can't really have a bigger hint can you? Thank you for giving me the opportunity to clear my head.

The poignancy of my encounter with Mairi was intensified by the fact that I have a daughter who is gay, whom I love very much. I find it incredible, in this day and age, that a lovely young woman should be driven to hurt herself simply for being who she is – especially when that unhappiness is fuelled by the sense that God is displeased with her.

I am happy to report that Mairi is now a confident, assured woman, comfortable with her sexuality and studying to be a doctor. She received help through her struggles – not least from the good Lord. But, fundamentally, she is where she is today because of her own choices. And she can be very proud of this.

Every one of us is the product of our choices – good and bad. But it's the bad ones that haunt us, leaving us with guilt and, sometimes, the after-effects of those choices. So here's the good news: no matter what we have done in the past, no matter what mistakes we think we have made, we have the power to do things differently. Like Mairi, we can ditch our bad choices and make new and better ones.

Some of my own not-so-good choices caught up with me a while back, resulting in a heart attack. I had known for some time that I needed to make changes to my life, but I slipped into thinking that this required some great level of resolve that I didn't have. However, what I discovered is that many of the great changes in life come not from gritting our teeth and trying harder, but from discovering new perspectives on our life and developing fresh patterns of thought and behaviour, one step at a time.

When Jesus called on people to change their lives, he told them to repent. This is now an unfortunate term conjuring up images of crazy people with banners saying 'The end is nigh!' It's a religious cliché associated with confessing our sins, or feeling really bad about ourselves, or trying to turn over a new leaf. However, none of this expresses what repentance really means.

The Greek word *metanoia* from which 'repentance' is translated literally means 'go beyond the mind' we have, or 'go into the large mind'. It suggests a complete refocus of attention, a double take, a different way of thinking that expands our outlook.

This is what happened to Mairi: she spent a whole year repenting – learning to think again, learning to enlarge her mind to accommodate a new identity, learning to ditch seeing herself as rubbish, learning to be kind to herself instead of wounding her precious body. Call it therapy, call it repentance – it's a change of mind, the beginning of a new and liberated experience of life, which I believe is always inspired and energised by God's Spirit.

Robert went through a similar but quite different mind-altering experience to Mairi. He was a guest at a wedding

I conducted. He introduced himself to me after the service in the midst of the dancing, drinking and merriment of the wedding reception. His face was slightly pale as he nervously told me about the strange thing that had happened during the service.

'I can't explain it,' he said, 'but somehow, during your talk, I felt like my whole life flashed in front of me . . . and it all seemed such a waste of time. Like I've been chasing all the wrong things . . . trying so, so hard to get what doesn't make me happy. It's all rubbish . . . I can see that.' He paused. Then through tears he said, 'Thank you! I think you've changed my life!' And he disappeared back into the crowd.

People's lives change as a result of all kinds of events and circumstances: through directly religious experiences, through counselling and therapy, through devastating turns of events, through a heart attack, through a conscious process of self-reflection, through a mysterious epiphany in a wedding service!

But the crucial turning point is when we start to look within, when we learn to reflect on our lives instead of just skating across the surface. This is when we can find out who we are, what we are about, what's important to us, what our core values are – the things that we would like to build our life on.

When our children were growing up, our deepest desire was for them to become the kind of people we would be proud of – not necessarily because of their academic achievements or career successes, but because of their character as individuals. Yes, of course we hoped they would share our Christian faith, but that would always be their decision. More importantly, we wanted them to be people with a functioning spiritual and moral compass, a capacity to make good decisions in life.

These guiding values are forged uniquely in each individual from qualities that are deeper and more fundamental than any creed or religious system – though they are embodied within all the great religious traditions. Qualities like love and compassion, patience, generosity, forgiveness, contentment, gratitude, a sense of responsibility, a sense of harmony and so on.

In my opinion, the best place to nurture and cultivate these qualities is within a faith community, but they are not 'denominational'; no faith tradition owns them. In Christianity, we call them 'fruits of the Spirit', and we find them supremely expressed in Jesus.

Bad Christians may struggle with much of the religious paraphernalia that surrounds the Christian faith, but their vision of life, the way they wish to follow, is based on the person of Jesus. Even at my lowest point with

Christianity – when none of the beliefs seemed to make sense, when I despaired at the sexist and homophobic attitudes I encountered, when I preferred the idea of being a pub landlord to that of being a vicar, when the church subculture drove me crazy – I still found the figure of Jesus compelling and inspiring.

There are many wonderful, godly figures within the world's religious traditions and beyond whom I admire and choose to emulate, but Jesus offers most clearly the model of humanity I most wish to follow.

So what does this mean in practice? How do we make good choices and ditch bad ones? How can we become the sort of person we want to be, the sort of person we, ourselves, respect and admire? Recent developments in brain science offer an encouraging answer and bring fresh substance to what repentance means.

Over the last twenty years or so, a revolution has taken place in neuroscience due to the discovery of something known as neuroplasticity. In earlier times it was believed that the brain is hardwired from early childhood; that adults have a set number of neurons performing functions in a particular way. It was also understood that the brain cells we lose on a daily basis could not be regenerated or replaced; once they were gone, they were gone!

But now it is known that the brain is malleable and

constantly changing, and that new neural networks can be deliberately created, giving us the capacity to develop new qualities, new habits, new abilities throughout our life – even into old age.*

Basically, when we exercise the muscles in our body, they get stronger. If we don't use them, they get weaker. It turns out that the brain is no different: we get good at things we practise. This doesn't just apply to things like learning languages or learning to play an instrument. We can actually develop our brains to help us be more compassionate or less greedy, for example.

If we practise lots of self-criticism, we develop the self-critical neural networks. Some of us are Olympic champions in self-criticism. But we don't have to stay that way. We can develop a new neural network that promotes self-worth and self-appreciation. How? By practice. Basically, we become good at what we practise. This applies as much to our brains as it does to the rest of our physical faculties. Mental habits – things we commit ourselves to – actually change the brain and make these actions and responses automatic.

So it's not good enough to say, 'That's the way I am. I

---

* See Norman Doidge, *The Brain that Changes Itself: Stories of Personal Triumph from the Frontiers of Brain Science* (Penguin, 2008).

can't help it!' We can change. We can develop new habits. We can make better choices in line with the qualities we admire and aspire to express. Surely this is what repentance really means: to change and expand the mind – to go beyond its present limits.

The key thing is learning to pay attention to our lives, instead of simply drifting through our days. If we don't pay conscious attention to our choices and how we wish to make them, our automatic pilot will kick in and take us down our well-worn paths, the old choices we wish to ditch.

Creating new pathways in the mind is a bit like making a new path through some woods: you just keep walking that way, as if there were a path, and before long the new path appears.

Developing spiritual or contemplative practices helps. I like the word 'practices'. It reminds me that life's greatest skills require constant rehearsal. We make mistakes. We screw up. We forget or get distracted. Then we start again. We become good at what we practise.

There are things in life that you can't change: certain circumstances, random events, the actions of others. There are other things that you can change. The Serenity Prayer, practised by Alcoholics Anonymous, offers a simple and profound perspective:

Laughing with God

God grant me the serenity
to accept the things I cannot change;
courage to change the things I can
and wisdom to know the difference.

I commend this prayer as a daily mantra and a spiritual
practice for life.

9. God is not a Christian

how to appreciate other religions without losing your own

God is clearly not a Christian. His concern is for all his children . . . that Christians do not have a monopoly on God is an almost trite observation.

– Desmond Tutu

When Amaka and Ansumana asked me to marry them, I knew we were in for something special. Amaka is a Christian, Ansumana a Muslim, and they wanted a wedding jointly conducted by a priest and an imam. Both traditions were to be honoured in the ceremony, both fully incorporated, with no cheap compromises.

The day turned out to be a magnificent convergence of religions, cultures, families and communities. Amaka's family is half-Nigerian, half-Indian; Ansumana's are from Sierra Leone. But both partners were born and grew up in Britain. So the three hundred guests at the wedding comprised a rich and diverse community of assorted backgrounds, connections, viewpoints and influences. If there had been any mind to fight about our differences, we had plenty to go at!

But this was a community of love and friendship, where differences were celebrated, not fought over. We were there to rejoice at the marriage of two beautiful people, but also to relish diversity and toast a partnership of difference. And to have a rocking good time in the process!

To add to the magic and extraordinariness of the occasion, the wedding took place in a marquee in a rural English village: hardly the obvious home for multi-religious and multi-cultural goings-on!

The wedding was more than a coming together of two people. It was also a marriage of two traditions and a merging of two wedding rituals – neither of which was lost in the process. Imam Alhaji from Sierra Leone, who lives and serves in South London, opened the proceedings with the Muslim marriage ceremony, quickly endearing himself to everyone with his humour, passion and humanity. Speaking warmly about the multi-faith nature of the occasion, he said that on a recent visit back to his home village in Sierra Leone, the first thing he did was to build a church.

Apparently, the Christian community there needed help with their building project, so he immediately mustered his Muslim friends and set about the task. When I chatted with him later about this, he simply said, 'That's what it's all about, Dave. We are brothers, we love one another.'

Many people's vision of religion was transformed that day. The congregation, which included Muslims, Christians and people of no faith in particular, witnessed a spectacle of religious harmony – the celebration of a multi-faith marriage, the warm working partnership of a priest and an imam, the mingling of different communities and traditions, and the demonstration that God belongs to no one and everyone.

How I wished I could bottle the spirit of Amaka and Ansumana's wedding to release it across our world, torn apart with violence, prejudice and terror, often in the name of religion. Yet I believe that this little event is simply a token of the aspiration of many people who loathe bigotry and intolerance and long for greater collaboration in creating peace on earth. As the Catholic theologian Hans Küng has said, there will be no peace among the nations without peace among the religions, and no peace among the religions without dialogue and greater understanding between them.

Perhaps the most important lesson we learned that day at the wedding is that humanity runs deeper than religion. The guests soon forgot about any difference among them and simply enjoyed each other's company. Being there, in that place, laughing, shedding a tear, wishing all the best for the happy couple, eating and drinking, chatting, sharing stories, soon made it obvious that we are all the same human beings. Our skin colour may differ, our customs and rituals may not be the same, our religious beliefs may vary, but we share a common humanity. We all bleed when we are cut, we all get hungry, we have similar fears and aspirations. The overwhelming majority of us desire to be decent human beings.

In his inspiring spiritual autobiography, the Dalai Lama talks about his three fundamental commitments in life: first as a human being, second as a Buddhist monk, and third as the Dalai Lama. How inspiring that his first commitment is not as a Buddhist, or a Tibetan, or as the Dalai Lama, but as a human being devoted to the enrichment of a shared humanity through mutual kindness and compassion. Religion, ideology, race and culture may divide us, but humanity brings us together.

The future of religion does not hinge on a theological solution, but on a human solution: we desperately need to create new stories of mutuality and hope that will generate a fresh spirit of fraternity and cooperation in building a more compassionate and sustainable world. In its own modest way, the wedding of Amaka and Ansumana is one of those new stories – for three hundred people, at least, who I hope will tell it and retell it, over and over.

The wedding also underscores that God is greater than any of our separate beliefs and traditions. God belongs to no one, and to everyone. There is no religion that can contain or define God. Of course there isn't! How could God be a Christian? Such a God would be hideously too small! God cannot be a Muslim, or a Jew, or a Hindu, or a Buddhist. God is not a tribal deity, but the Creator of the whole earth.

Every religious tradition affirms in some way that God is beyond the grasp of any of us: God is mystery, God is transcendent, God is the Great Beyond. As Muslims put it, '*Allahu akbar*!' It means not only 'God is great!' but 'God is greater!' Greater than our understanding, greater than any human idea of God.

Naturally, if we have spent our life imagining God to

be a Christian (or Hindu, or Jew, or whatever), it will be disturbing, disorientating – frightening, even – to entertain the idea that God belongs to others as well as us. But for Christians this should come as no shock; after all, two-thirds of our Bible (the Old Testament) is really the Hebrew Scriptures, where it is assumed that God is a Jew. And Jesus himself remained a Jew all his life, and showed no obvious inclination to create a non-Jewish religion. Christianity is, in fact, intrinsically a multi-faith tradition, a synergy of large aspects of Judaism with 'baptised' elements of other ancient religious and pagan cultures melded together around the figure of Jesus Christ and what he uniquely brings to the world.

However, the fact that God is greater than our faith tradition does not mean that our tradition is meaningless. Far from it. It simply underscores that all our visions of God are partial and cloudy. The best we can do is 'squint in a fog' or 'peer through a mist', as St Paul puts it.* No one has a clear view of God.

There's an old story about six blind people at the zoo feeling an elephant. 'Elephant is like a wall,' says one, stroking his side. 'No – elephant is not like a wall, elephant is like a rope,' says another, clutching the tail.

---

* 1 Corinthians 13:12 (*The Message* translation).

'A rope? No – elephant is like a sheet,' says the third, holding the ear. 'Elephant is like a soft, large hose,' says the fourth, grasping the trunk. 'No – elephant is like a tree,' says another, firmly wrapping his arms about a leg. 'Elephant is definitely like a solid pipe,' says the sixth, taking hold of the tusk.

We are all blind when it comes to comprehending the Divine. God is far greater than the vision of any of us. But, as I say, this doesn't mean that our meagre perceptions of God are invalid or untrue. I am a Christian. I am part of a tradition that understands God as revealed in Jesus Christ. This is my faith. It's how I know and experience God. I stake my life on it.

This leads us to another point, wonderfully underscored by Amaka and Ansumana's wedding: the need to appreciate and respect the faith of others without in any way retreating from our own faith. Thank God, the marriage ceremony of this lovely young couple wasn't some cheap amalgam of the two traditions, but a meeting of spirits comprising mutual respect and admiration. And on the wider stage, as we interact with people of other backgrounds, we are not looking for some bland religious pea soup where all our differences are dissolved, but for a vigorous dialogue where we can learn and evolve, yet still maintain the integrity of our own faith.

I have participated in, and enjoyed, many inter-faith conversations. I constantly read and listen to teachings and stories from other traditions. And I am enriched by all of them. However, my faith in Christ remains steadfast. I am not a Christian because I think Christianity is better than other religions; there are things in the Christian past and present of which I feel proud, and others of which I feel ashamed. I am a Christian because I continue to be captivated by the person of Jesus. There are many remarkable human beings in the history of all the world's religions, some of whom I admire massively; but for me, Jesus is the decisive revelation of God. He is the one I have chosen to follow. And it is out of my allegiance to Christ that I reverence the faith of others.

No one at Amaka and Ansumana's wedding had any desire to correct anyone else. From what I could detect, there was an avid curiosity and openness on the part of everyone towards the different views of others. We left feeling enriched and added to.

The great missionary E. Stanley Jones went to India in the early twentieth century and found himself overwhelmed by the depth of spirituality in that country. So instead of trying to convert everyone to Christianity, he set up 'round tables' – conversations between people of different faiths to share their experiences. No one was to argue or talk about religious theory. No one was permitted to pass judgement on another person's faith. No one could preach or try to convert the others, but were there simply to share their stories. Even agnostics and atheists were invited. 'Tell us what your agnosticism or atheism has done for you in experience,' Jones said.*

The essence of genuine discussion is that each person is open to the possibility of being changed by what is shared. Without this, we might as well stand in front of a mirror and talk to ourselves. So it follows that the object of interacting with people of different faith backgrounds is not simply tolerance of difference, but the expectation that our own faith will be enlarged by the encounter.

In the last analysis, our world needs more than mutual appreciation between the world's religious communities. It cries out for us to cooperate and work together with people of good will everywhere to make the world a more just and compassionate place. And we shouldn't wait for religious leaders and politicians to bring this about, but pursue it in simple acts of kindness in grassroots situations.

---

* E. Stanley Jones engaged in round-table discussions with Mahatma Gandhi, and wrote a biography of Gandhi, a 'portrayal of a friend'. And Martin Luther King Jr said it was this biography that inspired him to non-violence in the Civil Rights Movement.

When the members of Heartsong Church, just outside Memphis, Tennessee, heard that a new Islamic centre was being built next door, they put up a sign saying, 'Heartsong Church welcomes Memphis Islamic Centre to the neighbourhood.' And when they heard that the centre would not be ready in time for Ramadan, Steve Stone, the pastor, invited their neighbours to use the church for their prayers.

In post-9/11 America, this made national news. A group of Muslims in a small town in Kashmir saw reports about it on CNN and heard an interview with Steve Stone. After watching the broadcast, one of the Muslim leaders said, 'God just spoke to us through this man.' Another went straight to the local church and cleaned it, inside and out. In a message to Stone, one of the Kashmiri men wrote, 'We are now trying to be good neighbours too. Tell your congregation we do not hate them, we love them, and for the rest of our lives we are going to take care of that church.'

Although the Memphis Islamic Centre is now complete, the two communities work together every month to help the homeless in their neighbourhood, and there are plans to build a new friendship park that would sit on both congregations' properties, to blur the boundaries between the two religions.

This is another of those new stories of mutuality and hope we need to create in order to generate a fresh spirit of fraternity and cooperation that can end violence and hatred, and go about building a more compassionate and sustainable world.

Just before he was murdered, Martin Luther King Jr wrote,

> We have inherited a large house, a great 'world house' in which we have to live together – black and white, Easterner and Westerner, Gentile and Jew, Catholic and Protestant, Moslem and Hindu – a family unduly separated in ideas, cultures, and interest, who, because we can never again live apart, we must somehow learn to live with each other in peace.

More than forty years after King's death, we understand even more acutely the problems of living together in this great world house. And his words ring more true than ever: 'We must learn to live together as brothers or perish together as fools.'

In times of change and uncertainty, when familiar landmarks have shifted or disappeared, it is understandable that we hanker after familiarity and straightforward answers. But the future of our world hinges on 'round-table' people who will embrace diversity, upholding their own faith while affirming the faith of others, and working together to spread a global culture of justice, friendship and compassion.

10. Never mind heaven, what about now?

how to be at home in this world

*I am so absorbed in the wonder of earth and the life
upon it that I cannot think of heaven and angels.*
— Pearl S. Buck

Most of us have somewhere that feels a bit like heaven.
Mine is a ramshackle old cottage in a deserted valley in
Yorkshire. It's a mile from the nearest road, and throughout the twenty-five years that we have rented it, we have
forged a thousand unforgettable memories there.

When my friend Stuart, a Royal Marines chaplain, asked me to lead him on a spiritual retreat, we agreed that the cottage was the perfect place to spend the week. My wife Pat came along too – she would never miss a trip to the cottage, and she always has plenty of wise thoughts to contribute.

So we retreated up and down the valley each day with the dogs. And we retreated to the pub in the evening for food and sustenance. We spent time talking and reflecting and gazing at the hillside opposite. We prayed, and we kept silence in front of the fire. We also played the odd hand of cards and sipped some port.

On our last evening, after Stuart's wife Laura joined us, we decided to say prayers outside. It had been a lovely crisp autumn day and we'd had a fire outdoors all afternoon. By 5.45 p.m. it was dark, but still quite mild, so we huddled around the fire with just about enough of a glow to read our prayer books. As we prayed, two owls repeatedly called to each other across the valley and a delightfully slender quarter moon just peeped over the hill opposite – not bright enough to obliterate the gradual unveiling of the Milky Way overhead. It was one of those cherished moments when you feel completely at one with the surroundings, and so totally alive.

I would call it heaven. And it felt like home.

I am a lot happier with this kind of heaven than the mansion in the sky variety we sometimes hear about in church. I don't much like the sound of that heaven. I have no doubt that there is more to our existence than this mortal coil; I believe in something I call 'the beyond'. But I have no idea what this actually means. Nor does anyone I know. Not really. But I certainly don't believe in a heavenly holiday camp filled with harp-playing, hymn-singing and perpetual church services – or any other kind of everlasting torment!

I am more inclined towards the notion of parallel realities – the 'beyond' within the present, heaven all around. There is an old Celtic saying that heaven and earth are only three feet apart, and that there are 'thin' places where the distance is even less – places like our cottage. I reckon there are also 'thin' experiences, 'thin' moments, maybe 'thin' times and seasons, where the threshold between the two realities becomes more porous. This is surely what Halloween is really about: not trick or treat, or ghosts and ghoulies, but the sense of thinness between the realms of the living and the departed.

The kingdom of heaven, for me, is a state of consciousness – a different way of looking at the world, a transformed awareness that anyone may sense from time to time. Every truly joyful (I don't mean 'religious') experience is a taste of heaven. Every kindness is a taste of heaven. Every loving partnership, every real friendship is a taste of heaven. Every expression of beauty, every new discovery is a taste of heaven. Every selfless act, every attempt to create justice, every hungry mouth fed, every homeless person welcomed, every difference celebrated is a taste of heaven.

There is a stream of otherworldly spirituality within Christianity that tells us not to feel too much at home in this world; that we are exiles or aliens here, awaiting removal to our true home in heaven. I think this is mistaken. Yes, of course, there are things in the world that we shouldn't feel at home with – injustice, poverty, prejudice, greed, abuse, disease and the like – but it is these things that are alien and need to be eradicated, evicted and exiled.

We may feel at home in the world because God is at home here. God inhabits this material universe; he dwells within the dirt of planet earth; he can be found in the ordinary physical realities and activities of human existence. Isn't this what Jesus was getting at when he told his followers, 'The kingdom of God is among you'?* The world is God's house, God's body.

---

* Luke 17:21.

The object of religion is not to prepare us for the next life. It is a call to experience eternal life now, in this present world, in the ordinariness of everyday existence. Whatever comes next can wait. We will find out about that soon enough.

So how can we be more at home in the world?

First, it is essential to befriend our own body. Far too many of us feel dissatisfied or ill at ease with our bodies. We judge them harshly or try to ignore them. We treat them like slaves instead of the loyal friends they are, who support our hopes and dreams in every way they can. After I had a heart attack, I found myself putting my hand on my heart and apologising for the way I had treated it when it had served me so well for so long. I think we should talk with our bodies more often and more kindly.

But our culture does not encourage us to be kind to our bodies. We live under the tyranny of idealised notions of how our bodies should look and perform. Every day we are bombarded with visions of slim and beautiful people, and with advertisements for products that promise to recreate us in that image. But what if we resist? What if we dump the fake tan/nails/teeth/hair/boobs, the idea of a perfect backside, or rock-hard abs? What if we find the courage to love what we have instead of feeling the necessity to improve it? What if we didn't have to change anything about ourselves? Or what if we only make changes based on self-love?

It would be great if religion helped us to do this, to befriend our bodies. But sadly, Christianity has sometimes added to the problem, when the body is seen as an encumbrance to spiritual progress or a source of temptation to be beaten into submission. But we are embodied souls: our desires and appetites, our sexuality and sensual longings are part of our God-given identity to be embraced and relished, not disdained. If we are to be at home in the world, we must feel at home in the 'soft animal'* of our body and discover a spirituality of equilibrium, where every aspect of our humanity is valued and included, where we love and accept ourselves – including our bodies.

Second, we must learn to live in the present moment as fully as possible. It is so easy to be absent from our own life, preoccupied with thoughts and feelings that take us away from an awareness of life in the now. The reason my friends and I felt so fully alive on that lovely evening at the cottage was because we were fully present to what was going on. Anxieties, concerns, plans or regrets that might

---

* The term 'soft animal' appears in Mary Oliver's wonderful poem 'Wild Geese' in *Wild Geese* (Bloodaxe Books, 2004).

otherwise have occupied our thoughts were excluded. We were simply there, in that moment, at home in the world, present to the situation.

C. S. Lewis makes the point superbly in his book *The Screwtape Letters*, which details fictitious correspondence between a senior demon, Screwtape, and his nephew, a junior spirit called Wormwood, who is being coached in the art of troubling people and keeping them from connecting with God. To paraphrase, Screwtape tells Wormwood: 'Whatever you do, make sure you keep people as far from the present moment as possible. Get them to dwell on their past or focus on their future, but whatever you do, do not let them be in the present. The present moment is one of our worst enemies, for it is the closest thing to eternity people will ever experience and it is where God has the most opportunity to influence them.'

We cannot be at home in the world when we are engrossed in worry or anxiety, or when we are obsessing about the future or the past, or wishing we were somewhere else – wishing we were *someone* else. If we are not fully present, we cannot be reached by God's love and reassurance, for this is where God is: in the present. God is the eternal now. Jesus said, 'Look at the birds of the air; they neither sow nor reap nor gather into barns, and yet your heavenly

Father feeds them.'* Trust only operates in the present. There is a lovely part in Douglas Coupland's book *Life after God* where he says that birds are a miracle because 'they prove to us there is a finer, simpler state of being which we may strive to attain'.†

Third, we need to cultivate contentment. Contentment doesn't mean that we don't want things to be different or better. Contentment is the sense that we are on a journey, being who we are, doing what we can, and living in a way that is right for us now. It's a by-product of living according to our values.

So much around us conspires to make us feel discontent with our lives, to be ill at ease in the world: notions of happiness based on acquiring more and more stuff; images of perfect bodies, perfect partners, perfect lives that we can't attain; the sense that everyone else is doing so well and achieving their goals when we are not; the feeling that life is rushing by and we haven't even got started.

Contentment is an art, a state of mind that can be cultivated. Here are a few of my tips for increasing contentment.

---

* Matthew 6:26.
† Douglas Coupland, *Life after God* (Scribner, 1999).

Never mind heaven, what about now?

Make an inventory of things you are thankful for, or keep a gratitude journal for a couple of weeks or a month. And be sure to express your thanks.

Connect regularly with nature. Take walks in the park or the countryside.

Avoid comparing your life with other people's lives. Have the courage to just be you.

De-clutter your space and your mind wherever possible; keep life simple.

Have fun! Make room for gratuitous pleasure.

Spend lots of time with people who love you just because they do.

I make no apology for recommending, yet again, the Prayer of Serenity, which is the perfect prescription for a contented life:

> God grant me the serenity
> to accept the things I cannot change;
> courage to change the things I can;
> and wisdom to know the difference.

Ironically, the fourth way to be at home in the world is to be reconciled to our mortality. I have never found this very easy to do. I love my life. I want it to go on and on.

Sometimes people ask if taking funerals most weeks of my life helps me to deal better with my own mortality. Not really. However, it does leave me in no doubt that I am going to die one day. So I am forced to contemplate this.

We prefer to avoid talk of death. Apart from when we are dealing with the loss of a loved one, or attending a funeral, the theme of death is absent from most of our conversation. And once again, our culture does not help us, with its facelifts and anti-ageing drugs, its obsession with youthfulness, its avoidance at all costs of the subject of death. Where in our education system do we learn about death and how to deal with it? How often is it talked about in families? What parenting class helps us to discuss death with our children? There is no coaching, no pedagogy of death.

Julia is one of the people who always seems so at home in the world. Along with our long-serving church gardener, Sam Murphy, she cares for our communal garden and is greatly loved. Julia loves life. She's interesting, fun to be with, never short of a word of wisdom to share, and exudes a sense of calm. But she is dying. We are all dying, but she knows her time isn't too far away – though she has defied all predictions so far. Julia has inoperable cancer.

Apart from being a member of my congregation, she is a dear friend. And I love talking with her. One of the things I find most endearing about Julia is the way she talks about her departure in such matter-of-fact terms. I don't know what it does for her, but it is a therapy to me to discuss death in this way. It's a cliché, but being with Julia really does teach me the importance of living each day as if it were your last. Because that is how she is.

John O'Donohue, the stunning Irish writer who died a few years ago, aged fifty-three, includes in his book of benedictions a blessing 'For Death', in which he prompts us to ask how we can live the sort of life we would love to look back on from our deathbed.*

In his reassuring statement, 'Unless a grain of wheat falls into the earth and dies, it remains just a single grain; but if it dies, it bears much fruit,'† Jesus helps us to see that life is hidden in death. That bodies laid in the ground or scattered as ashes are really seeds; that somewhere just beyond our vision new buds are appearing, a new life is beginning to sprout.

No, I don't believe in the heavenly holiday camp, a *Hi-de-Hi!* eternity, but I do believe in a Beyond that is

---

* John O'Donohue, *Benedictus: A Book of Blessings* (Bantam Press, 2007).
† John 12:24.

already in our midst. We cannot envisage or anticipate precisely what heaven might mean in the future, but we can begin to experience it now. And we can place our efforts behind turning many people's present hell into something a little more heavenly.

11. Good God/bad God?

how to make sense of suffering

Life is difficult. This is a great truth, one of the greatest truths.

– M. Scott Peck

OK, I admit it: the title of this chapter is a bit of a swizz. I don't really know how to make sense of suffering. And, actually, I don't know anyone who does. People far smarter than me have written tomes on the subject without coming up with a satisfactory answer, so why should I fare any better?

Yet the question won't go away. How can it? Every day our screens are filled with heart-wrenching images and stories of meaningless pain and torment that we feel help-less to do anything about. Then there is our own suffering, and that of people we know and love.

Whether far away or close at hand, suffering is just horribly perplexing. 'Why?' 'Why them?' 'Why me?' 'Why anyone?'

However, the last thing we need – the last thing most of us want – is neat and tidy, smarty-pants answers, especially when we are in the very throes of dealing with a sudden death, a terminal illness, a pointless tragedy. I confess to entertaining homicidal reactions to people I hear spouting self-assured explanations for other people's misery, partic-ularly when it's spoken from a pulpit! The only response that makes any sense is silence, silent presence.

Yet the truly stunning thing, the most awe-inspiring, is the resilience with which so many people deal with suffer-ing and pain: people who doubtless feel anything but resilient on the inside, yet somehow carry on loving, giving and hoping in the face of personal desolation.

Take Marie, for example, a mother whose eyes tell me that she still hasn't recovered from the loss of her son Tony after seven years. He was a troubled soul, with a chaotic drug-taking lifestyle, who hung out with the wrong crowd. I knew him quite well, in a passing sort of way. He had a buoyant sense of humour and would often make playful 'vicar' jibes at me in the street.

Then, one day, Tony rang my doorbell and asked if we could talk. This time there were no jokes or jests. Weeping, he told me how much he would love his life to be different, but how helpless he felt to bring it about. He was intensely sad at the pain he caused his family, especially his mum. We spoke of God's love and forgiveness, and we prayed together. But the hill was too big for him to climb. A few weeks later, he went missing. His body was discovered after several days in a dark corner of a disused underground car park. He had overdosed.

Marie's mother-heart was broken. Not just because of her son's passing, but because of the thought of him dying alone in such a place. She was comforted when I told her about his visit to me, and his longing to change. I also said that I didn't believe Tony had died alone; that God was with him, nestling him into eternity where he could be the person he yearned to be. I shared with her that wonderful line from *The Cloud of Unknowing*, where the anonymous fourteenth-century writer says, 'It is not what you are or what you have been that God looks at with his merciful eyes, but what you desire to be.'

Tony's aspirations were also part of who he was; perhaps the truest and deepest part.

Seven years of suffering are visible in Marie's eyes. She will carry it to the grave. Yet somehow she presses on, bearing her grief, but being the mother the rest of her family need her to be. I don't try to find answers for people like Marie. The words would be unbearably hollow. And she doesn't need them. The strength of her spirit in the face of such sorrow is the best answer to suffering I know.

Elie Wiesel, the Jewish writer, tells one of the most moving accounts of struggling with evil and suffering in his book *Night*, which is a devastating account of his experience with his father in the Nazi concentration camps at Auschwitz and Buchenwald.

He recounts an episode where two men and a child are hanged in the camp before the eyes of the assembled prisoners. The men cry 'Long live liberty!' and die quickly. The child is quiet.

'Where is God? Where is He?' someone behind me asked.

At a sign from the head of the camp, the three chairs tipped over.

Total silence throughout the camp. On the horizon the sun was setting.

. . . The two adults were no longer alive . . . But the third rope was still moving; being so light, the child was still alive . . . For more than half an hour he stayed there, struggling between life and death, dying in slow agony under our eyes . . .

Behind me, I heard the same man asking: 'Where is God now?'

And I heard a voice within me answer him: 'Where is He? Here He is – He is hanging here on this gallows . . .'

That night the soup tasted of corpses.*

As the German theologian Jürgen Moltmann points out, Wiesel describes this horrifying reality in highly symbolic terms. The child is described as 'an angel with sad eyes'. The three murdered victims and the setting sun remind us of the death of that other Jew, Jesus, on Golgotha. But the soup that tasted of corpses does not point to any Easter. The answer to the question 'Where is God?' comes through 'a voice within me', like the voice of God in a prophet.†

But what does the voice disclose? What is Wiesel really saying about this alarming event? It can be interpreted in two ways. On the one hand, it may indicate that God is

---

* Ellie Wiesel, *Night* (Bantam Books, 1982).
† Jürgen Moltmann, *God for a Secular Society* (SCM Press, 1999).

the victim; that God dies there, once and for all, in the innocent child with the sad eyes. In other words, in the face of such horror, it is impossible to continue believing in God. Wiesel writes, 'I shall never forget the moments which murdered my God and my soul. I shall never forget the flames which consumed my faith for ever.'

The other possible interpretation is that God is present in the child's suffering; that where that child suffers torment, God also is tormented; where that child dies, God also suffers the child's death. 'If I make my bed in Sheol [hell], you are there,' writes the psalmist.* God was there, in the hell of Auschwitz, but not as the Almighty, the Lord of history, but as a victim among millions of victims. And the Jewish child did not die alone, was not forsaken by God. God suffered with him.

Elie Wiesel, summing up the story, concludes, 'We cannot understand it with God. And we cannot understand without him.'

I think both interpretations make sense in their different ways. When a father whose daughter had been raped and murdered cried out, 'Don't talk to me about God!' something deep inside me said, 'Yes. I agree.' But then I am also faced with the likes of Gordon Wilson, who held

---

* Psalm 139:8.

his daughter's hand as she lay dying after the Enniskillen bombing, whose faith in God was unshaken by what happened. Recounting her last words, 'Daddy, I love you so much', he goes on to say, 'But I bear no ill will. I bear no grudge . . . She's in heaven and we shall meet again. I will pray for these men tonight and every night.'

The most basic way to make sense of suffering is to be honest with yourself and God. Discover a religion of the gut, not of the mind. It's no use pretending, no use saying the 'right' words, no use contorting our emotions or simply trying to adopt a good 'Christian' outlook. We have to be emotionally authentic.

The book of Psalms in the Bible has been the prayer book of Jews and Christians for centuries. In many places it is shocking in its gut-wrenching honesty. Take Psalm 137, for example, which opens with the line immortalised by Boney M: 'By the rivers of Babylon – there we sat down and there we wept when we remembered Zion.' Don't let the catchy tune and the dance rhythm suck you in: Psalm 137 is a grumpy lament from an angry soul who has been abducted and forced to live in a foreign land. His anger boils over as he rails against his captors: 'Happy shall they be who take your little ones and dash them against the rock!' (You can see why Boney M chopped that bit out.)

But hang on. It wasn't us who were taken hostage; it

wasn't our children who were slaughtered by an invading enemy; it wasn't our homes that were looted and burned to the ground. Is this how the parents of the Moors murder victims feel? My liberal sentiments inclined me to see Myra Hindley, one of the convicted murderers, released before she died. But it wasn't my precious kids who were snatched away and brutally murdered, their fragile bodies buried in shallow graves out there on the cold, lonely Saddleworth Moors.

The book of Psalms doesn't just contain happy-clappy, sanitised religion; it voices moody, gut-level, fiery passion, honest to the core. 'Why, God?' is a common theme in the Psalms, along with variations on the question, 'Where the heck are you, God?' In the midst of pain it can be hard to make out where God is or where God stands. So sometimes prayer means having someone to shout at; at other times, someone to lean on; most times, a mixture of both.

But often God comes in the form of another person. It's a friend, a partner, a professional carer we shout at and lean on. Suffering can be very isolating; pain is deeply personal. So to discover a companionship of suffering makes a massive difference. And the point at which we choose to share our suffering can be crucial, not just for ourselves, but also for the other person who may long to be a part of our pain.

I learned long ago, however, both as a friend and as a vicar, that it is seldom advice that people look for or need in their suffering. Early in my ministry, a young father in the church died of cancer, leaving a grief-stricken wife and two bewildered young children. Shortly after his death, at the end of a service, his wife turned up at church. I felt I couldn't face her. I couldn't face her pain without something wise or profound to say that would make it better. So I looked busy and hoped she would talk to someone else. But our eyes met, and the next moment we were in each other's arms. She sobbed . . . and I cried. Then she looked at me and silently mouthed, 'Thank you.' Nothing needed to be said. A companionship of suffering may not make sense of the pain, but it halves it.

It also helps to recognise that most suffering is random. You don't deserve to be ill; the people of Southeast Asia did not deserve a tsunami; the residents of Christchurch did not deserve an earthquake. We live in a world where 'shit happens'! Yes, we sometimes do things, or other people do things, that cause suffering, but once we look at this in a simple cause-and-effect fashion, we are headed for trouble. Especially if it is linked with some notion of divine retribution in suffering – such as a ridiculous tele-vangelist suggesting that Haiti deserved an earthquake because it made a pact with the devil in practising voodoo.

The trouble is, if we believe in a transcendent God 'out there' somewhere else, 'up in heaven' deciding on some basis or other whether or not to 'intervene' in human situations, we have to take the bad with the good. The Almighty may decide to bless us with a nice new car, or alternatively, to let our son get killed in a car accident.

But what other kind of God is on offer? A disinterested deity, who winds up the clock, as it were, then lets it tick away on its own while he does something else? I believe neither in the 'fat controller' in the sky, nor in the nonchalant cosmic clockmaker. I'm more inclined to believe in a God who interacts with the world in love; who is radically involved with and embedded in our pain and suffering – the God who shares in the torment of the 'sad-eyed child', kindles in Marie the hope to carry on living, inspires Gordon Wilson to combat hatred with love and forgiveness.

Why do diabolical things happen? Why did my friends' seventeen-year-old daughter die in a car crash? Why are the people in the Horn of Africa cursed with yet another drought? Why did that little boy get cancer? Why are four million babies dying in the first month of their life? There are lots of answers to such questions. None of them help the victims or their loved ones very much. In my experience it is the onlookers who tend to ask, 'Why?' The people who suffer are more likely to ask where they can find help, or how they will manage. Ultimately, it is not an answer to a theoretical question that is required, but companionship: a God who shares our suffering and carries our griefs.

When the tsunami hit Thailand, I was interested to hear a local commentator say it was the people far away from the disaster who were questioning the presence of God. On the ground, he said, prayer was keeping so many people going.

The greatest challenge is to use our suffering to make the world a better place. Les Persaud is an amazing example of this. When his son Stefan was brutally murdered, he became disturbed by the anger and vengeance among Stefan's friends. So instead of drowning in his grief, Les found the strength to gather his son's hurting friends to help them build a better future. He pledged himself to mentoring them to reach their potential in ways his son never had. After five years, twelve have completed college (five going to university), two are training to be FA coaches, and none has fallen foul of the law.

Les and Stefan's friends still meet every Tuesday evening, and several of them have formed an enterprise called 'Potential' to give other youngsters what Les has drummed into them: the belief that life is all about making the right choices. They go into schools to give young people strategies for coping with knives, guns and gangs. Les lost a son, but became a father to many.

Victor Frankl, the Jewish psychotherapist and Holocaust survivor, spent three years in a concentration camp, living under the shadow of the gas chamber. He concluded that even in the most absurd, painful and dehumanised situation, life has potential meaning and that therefore even suffering is meaningful. But he argued that the human being is a 'deciding being'; that we may not be able to determine what happens to us, but we can decide how to react to what happens to us. Looking back on the dark days of his imprisonment, he wrote:

> We who lived in concentration camps can remember the men who walked through the huts comforting others, giving away their last piece of bread. They may have been few in number, but they offer sufficient proof that everything can be taken from a man but one thing: the last of the human freedoms – to choose one's attitude in any given set of circumstances, to choose one's own way.*

---

* Victor Frankl, *Man's Search for Meaning* (Simon & Schuster, 1984).

There is no satisfactory theoretical explanation for suffering. Why does God permit it? Jürgen Moltmann comments that any answer to this question that begins with 'because' makes a mockery of the sufferers and blasphemes God. We cannot answer the question in this world, but we cannot let it lie, either. We have to live with it, as with an open wound in our lives.

12. A wing and a prayer

how to talk to God

I don't believe in prayer; I only do it.

– Sam Keen

When Ben Kinsella was stabbed to death just around the corner from St Luke's Church, it shook the community – especially local young people. Ben was a popular sixteen-year-old, the life and soul of his class, who was out with mates celebrating the end of their exams when he was attacked and killed by a gang of boys. Ironically, he had written a letter to the prime minister as part of his English GCSE coursework, suggesting possible solutions to the recent spate of knife-related crimes.

A week after the killing, a candlelight vigil was held at 2 a.m., the time of Ben's murder, on the spot where the attack took place. It was a moving sight: hundreds of people, many teenagers, gathered on the corner of a North London street, bearing every sort of candle and lantern imaginable. The tears flowed as a community stood still in shock, the sound of murmuring not loud enough to mask anguished wails. Candles were lit, flowers laid, a minute's silence kept. Messages were written in black ink on paving slabs, and scrawled on white Arsenal Football Club shirts – even on some white knickers.

Summoned on Facebook, by any estimate this was a powerful prayer happening where a soulful litany of grief, anger and tribute found silent speech in petals, tiny flames, felt-tip ink and tears.

It wasn't a religious occasion, yet it was deeply religious. And heaven took account of this eloquent night offering.

Prayer is one of the most democratic activities I can think of. No one owns prayer. No one can dictate how prayer should be offered, or by whom. Anyone can pray:

anywhere, anytime, and in any fashion they choose. There is no right or wrong way to do it, no required formula of words. Words may not even figure. Prayer doesn't have to be said in a church or a mosque or a synagogue, or with any special functionary present. It is soul talk – the voice of our deepest, truest self, aired through whatever language or gesture we choose.

In her wonderful book *Eat, Pray, Love*, Elizabeth Gilbert describes her one-year spiritual odyssey, a 'search for everything', that took her around the world. The story begins with the breakdown of her marriage, and a scene where she is on the bathroom floor in the middle of the night, distraught and ready to do the unthinkable – pray! It's her first venture into prayer, so she's not entirely sure about the etiquette.

'Hello, God. How are you? I'm Liz. It's nice to meet you.'

That's right, I was speaking to the creator of the universe as though we'd just been introduced at a cocktail party . . . In fact, it was all I could do to stop myself saying, 'I've always been a big fan of your work . . .'

Gathering herself, she continues:

'I'm sorry to bother you so late at night, but I'm in serious trouble. And I'm sorry I haven't ever spoken directly to you before . . . I'm not an expert at praying, as you know. But can you please help me? I am in desperate need of help. I don't know what to do. I need an answer. Please tell me what to do. Please tell me what to do. Please tell me what to do.'

Her prayer tapered itself into this simple petition, 'Please tell me what to do', repeated again and again.

But after a while, she stopped pleading and sobbing and just heard this voice in her head. Not some special 'Old Testament Hollywood Charlton Heston voice', but her own voice, speaking as she had never heard it before: perfectly wise, calm and compassionate. 'Go back to bed, Liz,' it said. 'The only thing you need to do for now is get some rest and take good care of yourself until you do know the answer.'*

The bathroom floor was a turning point for Elizabeth Gilbert: a dark night of the soul, a moment of transformation. But she insists it was not a religious conversion, more the beginning of a religious conversation; the first words of an open dialogue that would bring her very close to God.

---

* Elizabeth Gilbert, *Eat, Pray, Love* (Penguin, 2006).

But what if we aren't sure about God? Can we still pray? Will it mean anything? Yes, absolutely. I think most of us already pray quite often, whether we think of it as prayer or not: the stammer of pain at someone else's pain; the sparkle of joy at someone else's joy; the silence within when something very beautiful is happening, or something very bad; whatever it is we feel when we sense deep longing or deep happiness. All this in its own way is prayer – the soul talking.

Someone I spoke with recently said that he couldn't quite bring himself to believe in God, and therefore struggled to tell his sick friend that he was praying for her. Yet he wanted to pray for her. So instead, he told her, 'I am having good thoughts for you.' Similarly, at Holy Joes (the church I led in a pub), I suggested that the people who struggled with conventional prayer language say, 'I wish . . .' instead of 'I pray . . .' This is essentially what a prayer is – a wish, a good thought, a feeling, a longing.

And whatever else it may be, prayer is an important way of talking with yourself. Don't knock it! I think it is very sad that we can go through much of our life without a decent conversation with ourselves.

I suspect this is what Douglas Coupland is getting at in his book *Life After God*, where his lead character says:

Sometimes I think the people to feel the saddest for are people who are unable to connect with the profound – people such as my boring brother-in-law, a hearty type so concerned with normality and fitting in that he eliminates any possibility of uniqueness for himself and his own personality. I wonder if some day, when he is older, he will wake up and the deeper part of him will realise that he has never allowed himself to truly exist, and he will cry with regret and shame and grief.*

Prayer is just this, a way of connecting with the profound – the deepest part of us, the part that yearns, and hopes, and delights, and hungers. Without touching this we simply skate over the surface of life. We don't allow ourselves 'to truly exist'.

Take Jim, for example, a man with his own business who constantly got into scrapes with employees and clients alike because of his hot temper. After engaging in some inner work with the help of the Enneagram, he began to deal with some of the reasons for his anger. He then developed a daily practice of leaving for work early and parking by a local lake for twenty minutes. Watching the swans and the progress of nature's rhythm through

---

* Douglas Coupland, *Life After God* (Scribner, 1999).

the year, he discovered an inner calm that transformed his life and relationships. Instead of a room clearing when he walked in, people wanted to be with him; his passionate energy converted from aggression to support. Jim isn't religious. But he prays every day, and is altered in the process.

Why not develop the habit: talk with yourself about what you have done, what you have failed to do; who you are, who you wish you were. Talk about the people you love, the people you don't love. Talk with yourself about the things that matter most to you. And listen to your hidden feelings about all these things.

Even if you don't believe anybody's listening when you pray, at least *you* are listening. But believe me, somebody is listening. Prayer is more than talking to yourself. As we open ourselves to the great 'within', as we express our concerns, our longings, our hopes and aspirations, we also open ourselves to God.

Does this mean that we should expect God to answer our prayers? Should we envisage miracles happening? Well, I have seen enough minor miracles in my life not to discount them. However, I don't think prayer is like ordering on the internet: you choose your product, then sit back and wait for it to arrive.

Frankly, I pray for people and situations because I don't

know what else to do. I cry out (sometimes literally) for my friend who is dying of cancer; I repeat mantra-like petitions, light candles and write requests on prayer boards. Do I think she will get better? Probably not. But I have to do it. It definitely helps me. And I'm sure it helps her too, to know that people are praying for her. As someone has said, 'Prayer was never meant to be magic . . . it's an act of love.' And who knows?

There have been various scientific experiments conducted to try to establish whether prayer is effective. The outcome is not entirely conclusive, partly because God may not necessarily wish to comply with the conditions of such trials. However, Dr Peter Fenwick, a leading British consultant neuropsychiatrist, concludes that there are sufficient studies now to show that prayer can work – to the extent that he thinks the presence of prayer groups in a hospital should be considered.

Essentially, prayer is an attitude of heart, so you can pray in any way you feel is right. Words are the most well-known means of praying, but I doubt that they are the most common. Prayer can find expression in almost any human gesture or activity – a gentle signing of the cross, an outstretched hand, a warm embrace, the lighting of a humble tea-light, a cup of tea, a scrawled message on a paving slab, the casting of a flower, an arm on a shoulder, an e-mail, a handful of earth thrown into a grave. When adoring parents passed me their baby at the font yesterday, that was a prayer. When the couple next door kissed before going to work, that was a prayer. When a surgeon feels compassion for his patient before inserting the knife, that is a prayer.

The seventeenth-century Carmelite monk Brother Lawrence left behind a collection of writings later published under the title *The Practice of the Presence of God*. Its constant theme is the presence of the divine in every part of life. God is everywhere, and everything can be an act of prayer.

Brother Lawrence confessed to being no good at set prayers. While he dutifully completed the three hours of prayer and meditation required of the monks, it was in mundane tasks that he really encountered God: baking pancakes for his brother monks, serving them wine, mending their shoes – these were the sorts of practices that prayerfully connected him to God. 'It is enough for me to pick up but a straw from the ground for the love of God,' he said.

One of the hardest practices of prayer is to learn to be silent. We live in a world of constant noise and chatter, with little space for quiet. Indeed, for many of us, silence is threatening; we prefer to surround ourselves with noise and avoid sitting still. But embracing silence is a way of opening ourselves up. This is what prayer is: the practice of opening ourselves to God, listening to our own heart, and being attentive to the pain and suffering of others.*

We may also see prayer as a form of co-creation with God. Not so long ago the world was envisaged as a big machine, and prayer required God to interfere with the working of things. But with quantum physics, the machine image has been replaced with an understanding of the world as a vast inter-connected network where small fluctuations at the quantum level can have dramatic effects elsewhere. Within this new picture, who knows the effect that prayer may have? If a butterfly flapping its wings in London can cause a hurricane in China, then might someone praying release energy for another person's healing? Call it quantum physics, call it mystery, call it prayer – I for one will keep on praying, keep on wishing.

---

* For specific practices of contemplative prayer and meditation, see Appendix 1.

13. Did God write anything else?

how to read the Bible and other good books

Never place a period where God has placed a comma. God is still speaking . . .

– Gracie Allen

Howard Thurman, spiritual advisor to Martin Luther King, tells a moving and revealing story about his grandmother and the Bible:

My regular chore was to do all of the reading for my grandmother – she could neither read nor write . . . With a feeling of great temerity I asked her one day why it was that she would not let me read any of the Pauline letters. What she told me I shall never forget. 'During the days of slavery,' she said, 'the master's minister would occasionally hold services for the slaves . . . Always the white minister used as his text something from Paul. At least three or four times a year he used as a text: "Slaves be obedient to them that are your masters . . . as unto Christ." Then he would go on to show how, if we were good and happy slaves, God would bless us. I promised my Maker that if I ever learned to read and if freedom ever came, I would never read that part of the Bible.'*

The preacher's text was in the Bible, sure enough. But the lady contested it. She believed that if the Bible didn't tally with her understanding of a God of love who created all human beings equal, then the Bible was wrong.

If truth is told, the Bible has been the servant of some pretty horrendous causes over the centuries. For one thousand four hundred years it was used to portray

---

* Howard Thurman, *Jesus and the Disinherited* (Abingdon Press, 1949).

Africans as cursed by God and to justify their enslavement. It was quoted to sanction witch-hunts in Europe and North America where tens of thousands of (mainly) innocent women were slaughtered in the name of God. It was drawn on to justify apartheid and anti-Semitism. And it is still used in various quarters to keep women subservient to men, to oppress gay people and to abuse the natural world.

That's quite a record for a book commonly labelled 'The Good Book'. Which simply begs the question: good for whom?

But there is another side to the story. The Bible has also been the basis of many important reforms in the world. As long ago as the fourth century it inspired Gregory of Nyssa to condemn slavery. In the nineteenth century it led people like William Wilberforce and John Newton to fight for the abolition of the slave trade. It has inspired people to contest poverty and injustice, to argue for equality between men and women. More recently, it has figured in all kinds of movements for justice, fair trade, peace and the care of creation.

Clearly, the Bible is used and abused to serve many different agendas – its power lying in the fact that it is seen to be the Word of God, which gives it a unique authority. Had Howard Thurman's grandmother revealed when she was a slave that she rejected what the Bible and the preacher taught, she would have been severely reprimanded – at the very least. Arguing with Holy Writ can get you into a lot of trouble!

But is the Bible the Word of God? Well, certainly not in the sense of God taking up pen and ink (or laptop and printer) and writing it. Nor did God dictate it to the writers, as fundamentalists believe. The Bible is a human book, written by fallible men who represented the limitations and preconceptions of their time and culture – and who had no idea that what they were writing would one day be considered Holy Scripture. The directive for slaves to obey their masters – just like Paul's other instruction for wives to submit to their husbands – is a reflection of the social attitudes of the time, and not the Word of God. Thurman's grandmother was right to argue with it.

So what are we to make of the Bible? Frederick Buechner gives a magnificent and unique assessment when he writes:

In short, one way to describe the Bible, written by many different people over a period of three thousand years and more, would be to say that it is a disorderly collection of sixty-odd books, which are often tedious, barbaric and obscure, and which teem with contradictions and inconsistencies. It is a swarming compost of a book, an Irish stew of poetry and propaganda, law and legalism, myth and murk, history and hysteria. Over the centuries it has become hopelessly associated with tub-thumping evangelism and dreary piety, with superannuated superstition and blue-nosed moralizing, with ecclesiastical authoritarianism and crippling literalism.*

A 'swarming compost' doesn't exactly sound complimentary – until we reflect that compost is the decomposing remnants of organic materials packed with rich minerals and natural fertiliser. On one level the Bible is a heap of leftovers, decomposing remains of ancient struggles to understand God in ways that seemed relevant at the time. We can't reconstruct that past, nor should we wish to, yet in our efforts to understand God afresh in our own age, we can draw on the rich spiritual nutrients from the past mediated through the 'disorderly collection' of documents we call Holy Scripture.

In my view, it is absurd to imagine that the Bible is literally the Word of God, or that it is, in any sense, infallible. And actually, the Bible never claims this for itself. The Bible is a collection of human writings about people who are both likeable and distinctly unlikeable, people who

---

* Frederick Buechner, *Beyond Words* (HarperSanFrancisco, 2004)

can be at one and the same time believing and unbelieving, who are saints and rogues, full of hope and full of despair – just like us. It's also a book about God – sometimes a God I find I can believe in; at other times one I can't believe in. Yet in the midst of its struggles, inconsistencies and contradictions, the Bible somehow speaks timelessly to our search for meaning and divine wisdom.

As the great Swiss theologian Karl Barth once put it, the Bible is 'pregnant with divine revelation': every time it speaks to me (which is often), the Word of God is 'born' again in my heart.

However, the Word of God is not limited to the Bible. Another of God's 'books' is the book of nature, often called God's 'second book' – though it was actually written first. Many people feel closer to God in nature than in church. I'm probably one of them. Nothing conveys the wonder of God quite like the Milky Way on a crisp, dark night, or like a common garden cobweb aglow with sunlit dew on a bright autumn morning. Even a family pet, like our dog Woody, can powerfully convey a sense of God's unconditional companionship. Nature lovers and scientists, each in their own way, are participants in the magnificent liturgy of the universe. As Galileo once commented, scientific curiosity is really an investigation of God's second book.

But the Holy Spirit is the inspiration behind many 'books' – whether religious texts such as the Qur'an and the Bhagavad Gita, or other spiritual writings such as Khalil Gibran's *The Prophet*, or music, painting, sculpture, poetry and mainstream theatre, films and novels. I have personally been overawed with divine presence at the Grand Canyon as well as the Yorkshire Dales. I have heard God in the golden voice and song-writing of Leonard Cohen, and my spirit has soared with holy excitement at a Faithless gig, listening to Maxi Jazz sing, 'This is my church. This is where I heal my hurts.'

Neither the Church nor the Bible has a monopoly on the Holy Spirit. God didn't start talking to us with the book of Genesis and stop talking with the book of Revelation. Divine inspiration is everywhere. Wherever hearts and minds are stirred to contemplate the depth and wonder of existence, wherever imagination transcends the mundane to glimpse beyond, wherever rumours of glory infiltrate human consciousness, wherever the dark night of the soul glimmers with hope, the Spirit touches us as divine inspiration.

Yet the Bible still has a unique place in Christian spirituality. It is the book of the Church, the classic text, which is fundamental to the shape and content of the Christian faith. But it is a strange book from a strange time and culture, which requires some skill and sensitivity to read and interpret.

The most basic requirement in reading the Bible is a willingness to wager that God loiters in and through its pages.

It would be stupid to pick up any book, or to watch any film or play without expecting that it may have something worthwhile to offer. Every time I purchase a ticket for a concert or a show, I wager that it will be time well spent. But a fruitful reading of the Bible calls for something more: the prospect that within its strange world something of crucial importance waits to be unearthed and interpreted.

I use the word 'wager' deliberately. The God of the Bible cannot be proven theoretically like some scientific fact. Nothing should be taken on blind faith (uncritically), yet we cannot progress without good faith (a genuine openness and receptivity to whatever or whoever may be revealed within and beyond the written page). The wager, then, is simple: that within the Bible's messy humanness, and despite its inconsistencies and contradictions, there lies a genuine testimony to the presence of the absolute in history.

I dare you to give it a go!

The second requirement is really an extension of the

first: a commitment to read the Bible both critically and receptively. These two elements certainly characterise my own relationship with the Bible. Over the years I have variously loved it and hated it, listened to it and ignored it, been irritated by it and captivated by it. I have sometimes felt like throwing it away, sometimes found it impossible to put down. It is, for me, both an intimate friend and a total stranger; a source of immense inspiration and the cause of constant annoyance. It is a push–pull relationship. Whenever I try to walk away from the Bible, I find myself inescapably drawn back into it. I am repelled by many sentiments expressed in its pages and by some of its portrayals of God, yet it also inspires and informs my highest and most treasured visions of who God is. And in a curious way it calls me, constantly, to be a better person than I am.

It's essential to ask searching questions of the Bible. For example, the passage where it says that the Lord told Moses to stone a man to death for gathering sticks on the Sabbath is too absurd for words. Perhaps Moses imagined that the Lord said this, but if it were true I would spend eternity ranting against such a hideous deity. A critical reading of such a passage encourages me to contemplate the evils of religious fanaticism still being performed in the name of God.

But it's easy to dismiss aspects of the Bible by crudely judging them in the light of present-day attitudes: for example, to assume that St Paul was a misogynist for expecting women to submit to their husbands. Leaving aside the critical question as to whether Paul really did write this, the fact is, first-century Christians cannot be expected to reflect a post-feminist vision of domestic relations. However, the deeper message of that passage is that the love of Christ should be the overarching ethic, which will lead husbands and wives to become one flesh and submit to each other.*

This helps to highlight a third requirement: treat the Bible as a source of wisdom, not as a book of instructions. Wisdom is concerned with the deeper meaning of things, not the mundane details, which are specific to particular times and cultures. We shouldn't look to the Bible to give detailed directions about life in the twenty-first century, or to offer straightforward guidelines on complex contemporary ethical issues that never arose in the first century.

Our society does not need religious laws and dogma. In a post-9/11 world, where fundamentalisms of every kind threaten global peace, we are all too aware of the dangers

---

* Ephesians 5:21–33.

of religious fanaticism rooted in perverse, literal readings of sacred texts. What we desperately lack today is wisdom – a way, a path of life leading to a spirituality of universal love and respect.

The Bible, like other religious texts, can add to or help to alleviate our problems. If it is applied in a literal, dogmatic fashion it will add to the factious discord of our broken world. We must draw on the wisdom traditions in our faith communities, discover a common global ethic and cooperate to bring healing and reconciliation to the world.

Some people may conclude that the Bible is too complicated or too contentious a book to bother reading – best just to leave it alone. But this simply isn't so. The practice of *lectio divina* offers an excellent way for anybody to start reading the Bible.

Don't be put off by the Latin: *lectio divina* just means 'sacred reading', or 'meditative reading'. It's the way that Christian monks have read the Bible for fifteen hundred years, and now lots of ordinary people are cashing in on the custom. It's really a way of praying the Bible, or chewing it over, that bypasses all the dogmatic interpretations. It is one of the best ways I know that anyone can tap into the wisdom of the Bible on a personal level.

The first thing to do is choose a short passage (3–6

verses) from the Bible and follow four steps: read, reflect, pray, contemplate.

The reading stage of the process needs no explanation. The second step is to chew it over in your mind: ponder the words; see how they make you feel; use your imagination to get behind them. Don't be afraid to feel confused by what you read, or to feel angry, or to be calmed by it. See if you can discover why you have these reactions. Put yourself in the story, in the place of the different characters. These are just a few suggestions; follow your own thoughts.

The third stage involves sitting with any emotions that arise and seeing if they shape up into a prayer. Don't worry if they don't. Remember, a prayer doesn't have to be words; feelings are prayers too.

Finally, the step of contemplation is where we become receptive to the spirit of the passage rather than its words. I have often found that this is where my attitudes have been transformed by the process, or where I have decided that I need to take some action as a result, or where I have simply spent time bathing in God's love or peace or reassurance.

So where should you begin? Let me suggest a few passages that would make a good starting place.

Psalm 23. The famous shepherd psalm by King David. This could be read in three sections: verses 1–3; verse 4; verses 5–6.*

Psalm 139:1–3, 4–6. God knows us completely and cares for us.

Matthew 5:9. Blessed are the peacemakers.

Matthew 6:9–15. The Lord's Prayer.

Mark 4:35–41. Jesus calms a storm.

Luke 6:32–36. Loving one's enemies.

Luke 9:46–48. True greatness.

Once you have tried out some of these, why not go through Mark's Gospel, a few verses at a time. This is the shortest and the oldest of the Gospels, but it also offers the most vivid account of the life of Christ. In the early part you will come across lots of extraordinary miracles. Don't get caught up with questions about how they happened, or if they happened – concentrate instead on what God may wish to say to you through them.

This is just the briefest of explanations of the practice of *lectio divina*. There is an excellent explanation of the practice and a guided exercise in Christopher Jamison's

---

* *I Shall Not Want* (SPCK, 2006) is a longer meditation that I wrote on Psalm 23.

book *Finding Sanctuary*.* Father Jamison featured on the BBC TV series *The Monastery*, where five very modern men volunteered to live the monastic life for forty days. It was a fascinating programme, and *Finding Sanctuary* is an excellent book that shows how aspects of the monastic life can be integrated into everyday experience.

What I like about the *lectio divina* method of reading the Bible is that it empowers ordinary people to make their own judgements about what the Good Book is saying to them. We began this chapter with a story about a slave woman (I wish we knew her name) who refused to accept the bit in the Bible about slaves obeying their masters. I will finish with a story from the Bible about a Canaanite woman who stood up to Jesus and even ended up changing his mind.

The Canaanites were traditional enemies of the Jews, so this woman was an outsider, a foreigner, and a woman too – a nobody – who came to Jesus for healing for her daughter. Jesus, speaking from a typical Hebrew perspective at the time, seemed to turn her away, because she wasn't a Jew, with an insulting comment about not feeding the children's food to dogs. 'Yes, Lord,' the woman responded, 'yet even the dogs eat the crumbs that fall

---

* Christopher Jamison, *Finding Sanctuary: Monastic Steps for Everyday Life* (Phoenix, 2007).

from their master's table.' Chastened by her comment, Jesus praised her faith and granted her request.*

Like the slave woman, this Canaanite woman (I wish I knew her name too!) refused to accept what was being said, even when it was Jesus speaking. Her instinct said that God was bigger than this. So she persisted, and got what she came for – converting Jesus in the process.

It's important that we too feel free to argue with what we read in the Bible. Sometimes, as we read, it may cause us to jump for joy; at other times it may make us boil with anger. Sometimes we are supposed to be angered by what we read – that is the point. At other times our reactions will change as we live with the passage or story for a while. A good reader is an honest reader. Don't be afraid to disagree. But also, never dig yourself into a position where the text in its very strangeness and awkwardness cannot finally change you.

The Bible is a window through which we hope to see God. The window is far from being entirely clear. It has fly specks, dust and the odd crack here and there that distract and obscure our vision. And it is only one window. But if we look through it, rather than at it, we may expect to glimpse the unimaginable wonder that we call God.

---

* Matthew 15:21–28.

14. Knock down the walls!

how to make church for everyone

> *Beloved community is formed not by the eradication of difference but by its affirmation.*
>
> — bell hooks

Once, a few years ago, completely by accident, I met my granddaughter. I should never have met her and it never happened again but just for a moment we looked at each other for the first and only time. We were completely speechless.

I've never met any of my other seven grandchildren or my two great grandchildren. My family won't allow me to see them. I've barely seen my three sons or my daughter in nearly thirty years. It's not that surprising: I raised my children to believe that someone like me is just not acceptable. So they don't accept me.*

This is part of the story of John who, along with his partner Mike, joined St Luke's ten years ago. John grew up in the Salvation Army and he loved everything about it: the music, the meetings, the whole way of life. Following in his father's footsteps, he became a bandsman, playing various brass instruments; then, later, he received the call to be an officer – the equivalent of what other churches would call a minister or priest.

From an early age John knew his feelings were for boys rather than girls, but he assumed this was normal, so, like everyone around him, he got married and had children. However, in John's case, this led to a terrible cycle of guilt, deception and confusion that lasted years. Eventually the truth about his sexuality came out, and this led to the loss of his marriage, his family, his career, his home and his life as a Salvationist.

---

* John's story, and others from St Luke's, are published in *The Gospel According to Everyone,* by Martin Wroe (lulu.com, 2011).

Even in his darkest times, John never felt rejected by God. However, his church and his family certainly did reject him. On learning of his homosexuality, his divisional commander demanded his instant resignation. Later his oldest son, now himself a Salvation officer, wrote to him saying that he was no longer his father and that he did not want him to visit him and give his children AIDS.

Early on in their time at St Luke's, John and Mike came to a service on Mother's Day, when, as it happened, a lesbian couple, Becky and Jude, brought along their four-day-old baby girl. As is my custom when a baby is brought to church for the first time, I took Izzy in my arms to welcome her and bless her in Christ's name, first gathering the other children around to give them a good look at her.

'This is Izzy,' I said. 'She's really lucky. Do you know why? She has two mummies!'

There were ear-to-ear grins, and one little boy exclaimed, 'Wow!'

John and Mike turned to each other, eyes filled with tears. 'I never believed I would hear such a thing in a church in my lifetime,' Mike commented later. 'When you said that to the kids, we knew we had come home.'

John and Mike recently became civil partners – on

John's seventy-sixth birthday! The moving ceremony closed with a recording of Leonard Cohen singing 'There ain't no cure for love'. As we listened to the golden voice, I just wished I had been allowed to conduct this ceremony at St Luke's.

Incidentally, John's encounter with his granddaughter occurred at a Salvation Army conference where he mentioned to a Scandinavian officer that his son lived there. To John's amazement, the officer said, 'I've brought his daughter with me.'

'And there she was,' John said. 'For a moment I looked into the eyes of my own granddaughter. Both of us lost for words. I've no idea what she'd been told about me . . . Even on my deathbed I'd love to see my children and grandchildren, just once, that is my desire, I'd love to see them. But it's all in God's hands.'

Astonishingly, Gene Robinson, the first openly gay priest to become a bishop in the Anglican Communion, received death threats and was advised by the FBI to wear body armour under his vestments at his consecration. His appointment led some conservative Episcopalians to form their own church.

However, shortly after his election as bishop, Gene got

a special greeting from an eighteen-year-old woman who was in prison for murdering her mother three years earlier. She wrote, 'I am neither gay nor Christian, but there is something in your election that makes me believe there is a community "out there" who might love me, despite what I've done.'

In this woman's eyes, a church choosing an outcast as its leader offered hope that she could be accepted as a human being despite her heinous crime. As a result of meeting her, Bishop Gene now spends every Christmas Eve in the prison. He says it is his Christmas present to himself. 'Why does my relationship with these women mean so much to me? Part of it is that when I'm with them, I feel closer to Jesus. It's not easy to feel close to Christ when you're sitting in a committee meeting or signing papers at a desk. But when you're doing the things Jesus did with the people he did them with, it's a whole different story.'*

I can't help wondering what sort of Church Jesus envisaged. If I believed for one moment that it was a place that had no room for the likes of John and Mike, or Gene Robinson, or a woman who murdered her mother, I would want no part in it. But I don't believe this.

---

* Gene Robinson, *In the Eye of the Storm: Swept to the Centre by God* (Canterbury Press, 2008).

I wonder how much of the Church Jesus would now lament – which 'tables' he would overturn. I even wonder if Jesus envisaged the Church at all. It has been said that what he preached was the kingdom of God; what he got was the Church! Fair comment. Throughout the Gospels, Jesus only uses the word 'church' on two occasions, while voicing the terms 'kingdom of God' and 'kingdom of heaven' over one hundred times. Clearly, the kingdom of God, not the Church, was his passion.

But what is the kingdom of God? Quite simply, it is a vision of what the world would be like if God were king instead of the rulers and politicians. Jesus taught us to pray: 'Your kingdom come, your will be done on earth as it is in heaven.' The kingdom of God appears wherever God's will is accomplished: wherever justice and fairness prevail, wherever hungry mouths are fed, wherever the homeless are housed, wherever reconciliation replaces conflict, wherever love wins out over hatred and revenge.

One of the most vivid and inspiring portrayals of the kingdom of God appears in Martin Luther King's notion of 'the beloved community'. In the face of bigotry and racial hatred, King dreamt of a transformed world: an integrated society, where brotherhood and sisterhood would be a reality; where people would not be judged by their creed, or gender, or by the colour of their skin, but would be accepted for who they were. He called this the beloved community: a companionship of love and justice.

Surely, this is why the Church exists: to be a living, breathing demonstration of the beloved community; to be a place of unconditional acceptance, a place of equal opportunity, a place where diversity is celebrated, where anyone and everyone can be at home in the love of God.

Jesus generated beloved community wherever he went. To him, 'church' wasn't so much a noun as a verb: it was an event, a happening, an experience, not an institution or a religious club. Basically, Jesus went about churching it – he did church: he befriended people across social barriers, included the untouchables, empowered the weak and underprivileged, utterly destroyed any sense of 'us' and 'them'. Wherever Jesus was, beloved community sprang up around him.

And especially over meals . . .

Nothing sums up what Jesus was about more fundamentally than his so-called 'table fellowship', where he shared food and drink with all kinds of people, particularly the outcasts of his day. It is impossible to exaggerate the impact these meals must have had upon the poor, the marginalised and the so-called 'sinners'. By sharing a meal with them, by treating them as friends and equals, by giving them somewhere to belong, Jesus lifted their shame, humiliation and guilt and replaced it with dignity, respect and self-worth.

In his ragtag community, Jesus radically reframed people's lives within the love of God. And this, more than anything else, is what the Church is meant to do: enable people to see their lives through the lens of God's loving presence. A woman said to me recently, 'The reason I come to church is to remind myself that I'm not rubbish. Right now, my circumstances are rubbish, but being here helps me to see that that is not me.' An enormous amount of my time as a parish priest is spent trying to let people see themselves as God sees them: to know that God is smiling at them, not frowning.

When I look at the St Luke's community each Sunday, I see a woman who has struggled long and hard with the 'demons' of mental illness; I see a man who spent years wrestling with guilt over a ruined relationship; I see a young woman who suffered nightmares after being raped; I see a friend dying of cancer; I see several people desperate for work; I see a couple who long to conceive; I see dozens and dozens of people just getting on with their exciting or humdrum lives. But I also see people able to view their suffering, their joys and their ordinariness through the lens of God's love in the Christian story retold in some way, week after week, in services. I see people who know that whatever they experience, they will never be quite alone ever again.

Church is meant to be a place where we discover unconditional acceptance. Being embraced within the beloved community does not hinge on believing the 'right' things, or conforming to some image of a good Christian, or managing to live a squeaky-clean life, or fitting some neat category of 'normality'. We are accepted because God – who knows us inside out – loves us, come what may.

In his day, Jesus smashed through the barriers that divided people. He befriended the detested Samaritans, even telling a famous story in which the hero was a Samaritan; he received correction from a Gentile woman; he even welcomed an occupying Roman centurion and healed his servant.

One of the most important ways in which the Church needs to manifest God's unconditional acceptance is in the Eucharist or Holy Communion. Based on Christ's practice of cutting across all barriers and sharing meals with every sort of person, I believe the holy sacraments should be offered to every person, without exception. The bread and wine are powerful signs of divine inclusion, which no one should be refused. Divine acceptance is not on the basis that we hold certain beliefs, or attain some moral standard, or become members of an institution, but simply on the grounds of Christ's hands open to all.

Church is also meant to be a celebration of diversity, a safe space for people to be different. Any church where everyone looks the same, believes the same things and behaves in the same way is a sorry expression of the beloved community, where difference is not simply tolerated but extolled.

One of the oldest metaphors for the Church is as the body of Christ, where each member, each organ, is different, yet contributes in that differentness to the whole expression of Christ in the world. In the beloved community there is room for every culture and race to be valued, room for women and men to work together as equal partners, room for gay and straight people simply to be human beings, room for different opinions and points of view, room for doubt and questions, room to change.

Finally, the Church is meant to be a community of empowerment, where wounds can be healed and souls are free to flourish.

We don't turn up at church because we are scrubbed-up perfect human beings; we are a gathering of broken people seeking to become whole – but seeking wholeness together, rather than alone. We are a mishmash of believers, doubters, dissenters and malcontents, each of us grappling our way towards the mystery that is God.

The Church is a place of refuge and hope, a place of prayer and laughter, a place of dreams and fresh imagining, a place of birth and rebirth, a place of welcome and acceptance, a place of weddings and funerals, a place where proud mums and dads bring tiny people to offer them to God, a place of parties, a place of bread and wine shared by all, a place of affirmation and new beginnings, a place of friendship, support and healing.

Of course, as I said in chapter 2, you don't need to look for God in some special place, whether a church, a mosque, or a temple. God is radically present with you everywhere, closer even than your breath. Yet take it from me, it is intensely satisfying to be part of a community of people who, week by week, choose to put themselves in a place where they are exposed to the distinct possibility that they will bump into God.

15. The quiet revolution

how to help God change the world

*How wonderful it is that nobody need wait a single
moment before starting to improve the world.*

— Anne Frank

When I agreed to take Carol's funeral, the undertaker
told me there would be only four or five people at the
service. She was a forty-five-year-old feisty Nonconformist
who grew up in a sleepy village in Bedfordshire, to which
she seldom returned. She drank heavily and developed a

heroin addiction, though she recovered from the addiction some years before her death.

When I spoke with her father on the telephone, he said he couldn't tell me a lot about Carol's life. He knew her as a rebellious teenager, a substance abuser and a misfit. He was aware that she lived in London and worked in a charity shop, but that was about it. He confirmed that the congregation in the crematorium would be small: him and his wife, plus two other relatives. I felt sad that I knew so little about Carol, and that her passing at a mere forty-five years of age was so uneventful.

As I walked from the car to the crematorium chapel the following day, I noticed thirty or forty people standing a little way from the building, chatting and rolling cigarettes. The cortège wasn't expected for another fifteen minutes, so I decided to speak with the group – who turned out to be Carol's friends. Within a few minutes, I had a completely different picture of her, and a quite different story to tell.

Almost all of the group were volunteer workers in charity shops in North London, a ragtag bunch of Goths and punks, along with a few more conventional types. One after another they eulogised Carol. One man in his early thirties with spiky black hair, a tattooed face and countless piercings said, 'Most of us have problems, man.

But Carol was like a mother to us. She gathered us in and looked after us.' Another man, who I later discovered was her shop manager, asked if he could speak in the service, where he talked movingly of Carol's maternal qualities. 'The charity shops are our family,' he said. 'A lot of us have mental health issues, but we've found a community where we can belong. Carol loved a drink, and she was always the last one dancing at 4 a.m., but she was the heartbeat of this family. She looked after everyone.'

Carol's parents were mild-mannered, middle-class folk. I wondered how they would react to the funeral of their prodigal being gatecrashed by a bunch of apparent dropouts and misfits. The couple thought they knew who their daughter was: a flaky waster, a drug addict and an alcoholic – but now they heard about a completely different woman.

'I wish I could meet her now,' her mum told me afterwards. 'We had no idea what a wonderful person she had become, or that she was part of such a loving family.' Outside the crematorium, Carol's dad went across to her friends and said, 'We planned to take Carol's remains back to Bedfordshire, but now we feel she should stay here with you in London where you can all visit her regularly and easily.' The hugs and tears that followed between a reserved out-of-town couple and a bunch of urban castaways was a sight to behold.

Carol's name will not appear in any list of saints, yet I drove home that day feeling I had buried a broken Christ-figure.

Jesus said, 'Truly I tell you, just as you [cared for] one of the least of these who are members of my family, you did it to me.'* Although Carol probably didn't realise it, she was a servant of God, who in her modest, unselfconscious way changed the world. She definitely changed the world of her little flock of walking wounded. She also challenged my idea of where to look for Christ in the world.

Joan Osborne's song 'One of us' hits the nail on the head, asking us to imagine what it would be like if God were just like us – a stranger, a passenger on a bus, someone simply trying to find their way home.

What does it do for our vision of God if we start to look for Christ in someone like Carol, or in the folk she cared for – people we may pass on the street without noticing that they exist? Yet isn't this what Jesus meant when he said, 'Just as you cared for one of the least of these, you did it to me'?

In some ways, Jesus himself was an unlikely Messiah. Virtually his entire life was spent in a political backwater among peasant folk; he had no obvious plan to change

---

* Matthew 25:40.

176

the world, no strategy to overturn the system, no programme for creating social change. Yet he did change the world – by changing the lives of, mostly, uninfluential individuals.

As we have seen, Christ's passion was the kingdom of God: a vision of what the world would be like if God were king instead of the rulers and politicians. But even here, he did not try to introduce the kingdom as a political strategy or programme. Rather, he went about spreading a culture of hope and compassion and healing among ordinary people. He broke down prejudice and social barriers, and empowered the poor and the marginalised: not in order to turn them into a militant force to overthrow the authorities, but in order to generate the beloved community.

The way that Jesus went about changing the world resembled what is nowadays known as the 'butterfly effect'. This is the principle that a small change in one place may have a dramatic effect elsewhere. The idea of the butterfly effect began when Edward Lorenz, a meteorologist, tried to explain in the early 1960s why it is so hard to make accurate predictions about the weather. He realised that small differences in dynamic systems such as the atmosphere can trigger vast and often unexpected results. In 1972 he presented his findings in a paper entitled

'Predictability: Does the flap of a butterfly's wings in Brazil set off a tornado in Texas?'

Lorenz's proposal appeared preposterous, but his ideas were shown to be completely true and accurate. The phrase 'butterfly effect' refers to the idea that a butterfly's wings may create tiny changes in the atmosphere that set off a chain of events that can, for example, ultimately alter the path of a tornado, or influence its speed, or have an impact on other weather patterns.

One of the applications of the butterfly effect is the recognition that decisions or actions we as individuals take, no matter how small, can play a massive role in determining the outcome of our lives and the lives of others – even entire cultures. This is why Gandhi's famous quote, 'Be the change you want to see in the world', is so powerful. It shows how one decision to change our personal world or the world of one other person can end up transforming a society.

In 1955 in Montgomery, Alabama, an African-American woman called Rosa Parks decided she was tired of having to give up her seat to a white person on a bus. She was not the first to take a stand, but her small act of defiance became an important symbol of the Civil Rights Movement. At a meeting a few days after her arrest, a mostly unknown church minister, Dr Martin

Luther King Jr, was elected as president of the Montgomery Improvement Association. And the rest is history – triggered by one woman's decision to act, a flap of a butterfly's wings.

Desmond Tutu says that the biggest defining moment of his life came through an unbelievably simple act of courtesy he witnessed when he was a young boy of nine or so. 'I saw this tall white priest in a black cassock doff his hat to my mother who was a domestic worker.' Tutu didn't know that the priest was Trevor Huddleston, a dedicated anti-apartheid activist. But he saw something he says blew his mind, and instilled in him a passion to pursue justice for black people. A miniscule flap of a butterfly's wings prompted a chain reaction that helped produce one of our world's greatest moral leaders.

Desmond Tutu declares that God has a dream that we can help turn into a reality: a dream of a world 'whose ugliness and squalor and poverty, its war and hostility, its greed and harsh competitiveness, its alienation and disharmony are changed into their glorious counterparts, when there will be more laughter, joy, and peace, where there will be justice and goodness and compassion and love and caring and sharing.'*

---

* Desmond Tutu, *God has a Dream: A Vision of Hope for our Time* (Rider, 2004).

Carol didn't care for her little family of misfits in order to change the world, any more than Trevor Huddleston doffed his hat to a black domestic worker to overthrow apartheid. Rosa Parks had no idea that her refusal to stand would inspire a movement to combat racial discrimination. Each of these people simply did what came naturally in the situation. They flapped their wings.

So how do we go about flapping our wings? How can we make a difference? Here are my top six tips for changing the world.

1. Don't try to change the world – be true to yourself

Before entering the public arena, Jesus spent forty days in the desert deciding who he was and who he wanted to be in the world. He didn't do things simply to please others, or to fulfil some ambition to be the saviour of the world; he was simply true to his deepest and best instincts. If you are true to yourself, you will change the world, because the world around you will change.

2. Commit to compassion

Compassion isn't feeling pity, or feeling sorry for someone, but a commitment to putting yourself in somebody else's shoes, to feel his pain or enter generously into her point of view. This is summed up perfectly in the so-called 'golden rule': 'Do unto others as you would have them do to you.' Compassion arises from an openness of heart, a willingness to understand other people's pain, to listen to their hurt and share in their distress.

The golden rule is at the heart of all major faith traditions. It's the mark of authenticity. 'Without love I am nothing,' says St Paul. But love isn't a feeling we wait to experience; it's a practice we commit ourselves to pursue and cultivate.

The Charter for Compassion is an initiative to restore compassion to the heart of religion and morality. Crafted by leading thinkers and activists in all the major faith traditions, it calls for a commitment to practise compassion in our daily lives. Visit the website today, sign the charter, make a commitment to act, and read some splendidly encouraging stories of compassion.*

Every single act of compassion is a flap of a butterfly's wings. You may not see the final outcome, but keep flapping!

---

* The Charter for Compassion was launched in 2009 by Karen Armstrong, who was granted a wish for a better world by TED (Technology, Entertainment, Design), a non-profit organisation devoted to Ideas Worth Spreading. She chose to create the charter with TED's support. Visit the website at www.charterforcompassion.org, make a commitment, get involved.

3. Join with others in seeking to promote justice and peace in the world

There is a statue in Rome of Christ without any arms. It's a wonderful symbol of how God relies on us to do his work in the world. Without human partners, God has no ears or eyes, no arms or legs. God is reliant on human cooperation in making the world a better place. Thankfully, there are many people involved in this work, not all of them Christians, not all of them religious. Indeed, millions of people of all faiths and none are working to combat poverty and disease, to feed the hungry and liberate the oppressed. And they are making a difference. But the need is massive. More people are needed to volunteer time and energy, to give financial support, to sign up and be involved.

In Appendix 3 I have listed some of the organisations and campaigns you might wish to consider joining or supporting.

4. Attend to the present moment

Pay attention! I can still hear my schoolteachers barking it at me. I was easily distracted, you see. Which is probably why I took a while to wake up, academically. I was always day-dreaming or thinking about playing football when school ended.

However, these are two of the most important words in the world: *pay attention*. Most of the great figures in history changed the world when they paid attention – to their own passions and longings; to some aspect of the world around; to the needs of another person; to some small detail in life; to God's voice in all of these things.

But in order to pay attention we need to be present in the moment. Gandhi once said, 'I do not want to foresee the future. I am concerned with taking care of the present. God has given me no control over the moment following.'

We all experience resistance that stops us from acting to change the world – to change someone's world. The best way to overcome this is to stay present in the moment as much as possible, to do what we can now instead of either wishing we had done more in the past, or trying to plan for the future.

I return, yet again, to the wonderful Prayer of Serenity:

> God grant me the serenity
> to accept the things I cannot change,
> courage to change the things I can,
> and wisdom to know the difference.

Sometimes it may seem that the things we can change are so small and minimal. But take courage. Beat your wings and leave the rest to God.

5. Overcome evil with good

Throughout history, many famous and completely anonymous people have taken up St Paul's challenge, 'Do not be overcome by evil, but overcome evil with good,'* and each of them has changed the world in some way.

In May 2008, sixteen-year-old schoolboy Jimmy Mizen was murdered by another teenager in a bakery in South London. Speaking about the killer, his mother Margaret Mizen refused to respond with hatred or anger. 'I don't feel anger because I know that it was anger that killed my Jimmy,' she said, 'and I won't let anger ruin my family . . . There is too much anger in this world and it has to stop.' She also spoke with compassion towards the killer's parents. In the face of cruelty and loss, the Mizens chose to overcome evil with good.

Two years later, the Mizens went further in their efforts to defeat the evil circumstance that took their son. In November 2010, Barry Mizen announced that they were buying the shop where his son died to open the Café of

---

* Romans 12:21.

Good Hope. The café, a 'community hub', serves sandwiches and handmade chocolates made by Jimmy's older brother, who is a trained *pâtissier*. Two other brothers are involved in running the café, and the profits go towards various charitable projects. The Mizens have also set up a website, familiesutd.com, to offer support to other families who have experienced violent death.

In a similar vein, Susan Retik, who was expecting her third child when her husband David was killed in the 9/11 attacks, refused to be eaten up by grief and bitterness. Instead, along with Patti Quigley, another 9/11 widow, she established a foundation dedicated to transforming the lives of thousands of Afghan widows, who are among the poorest and most destitute women in the world. 'Beyond the 11th', the two women say, is an initiative that transcends acts of hate with acts of humility, acts of despair with acts of ingenuity, and acts of fear with acts of self-reliance. 'We are helping to spread peace hand to hand and heart to heart, one widow at a time,' they say.

These are remarkable stories, but every single act of love or peace or forgiveness constitutes a beating of wings that will create waves and reverberations, however invisible or anonymous they may be.

6. Look for Christ in the world

When my good friend Mike Riddell pastored a church in Auckland, New Zealand, he had regular visits from Arthur, a man suffering with mental illness. Arthur used to tell Mike that he was the second son of God. One day, Mike got to thinking, 'What if it were true? What if Arthur were the son of God? What if God appeared as a mentally ill man?' And this prompted Mike to write a novel based on Arthur's story, called *The Insatiable Moon*.

The book, now an award-winning film, poignantly explores the question, while also challenging our preconceptions about mental illness.

There are many Christ-figures in the world, just as there are a million Christ-epiphanies – people and moments where God appears afresh in our world. None of these eclipse the unique revelation of God in Jesus, but they remind us that God constantly shows up in the most surprising places, through the most unexpected people.

And that includes you!

We all make choices every moment of every day that can in some way change the world for the better – if we choose the pathway of love and reconciliation rather than anger, selfishness, revenge or indifference.

The great twentieth-century theologian Paul Tillich wrote:

Death is given no power over love. Love is stronger. It creates something new out of the destruction caused by death; it bears everything and overcomes everything. It is at work where the power of death is strongest, in war and persecution and homelessness and hunger and physical death itself. It is omnipresent and here and there, in the smallest and most hidden ways as in the greatest and most visible ones, it rescues life from death. It rescues each of us, for love is stronger than death.*

Beat your wings, friends; this is the quiet revolution.

---

* Paul Tillich, *The New Being* (University of Nebraska Press, 2005).

16. It's over to you!

how to be the person you were born to be

Your time is limited, so don't waste it living some-one else's life. Don't be trapped by dogma – which is living with the results of other people's thinking. Don't let the noise of other people's opinions drown out your own inner voice. And most important, have the courage to follow your heart and intuition. They somehow already know what you truly want to become. Everything else is secondary.

— Steve Jobs

It's never too late to be what you might have been.
— George Eliot

The management guru Charles Handy tells the story of Luke, a young Afro-Caribbean man who, twelve months earlier, had been down and out and living in London. He had no job, no home, no money and no hope. There seemed to him to be little point in living.

Yet by the time Handy met him, Luke's life was transformed; there was no trace of his down-and-out past, no sign of defeatism or depression. He was enrolled in a college and was upbeat, charming, interesting in his views (they met at a conference on the future of work) and fully engaged with life.

'What happened?' Handy asked.

'Well, when things were at their worst,' Luke explained, 'I rang my dad and told him how I felt. All he said was, "Think about this: when you get to heaven you will meet the man you might have been." Then he put the phone down. That was all I needed. I went away, thought about it, and applied to the college.'*

I have to admit, the prospect of one day meeting the

---

* The story is from Charles Handy, *The Hungry Spirit: Beyond Capitalism, A Quest for Purpose in the Modern World* (Random House Business, 1998).

person that I might have been is pretty scary, but as Handy says, you don't need to take this literally to get the point. In that moment on the telephone Luke saw his life in perspective, realised it didn't have to be that way, and did something about it. He turned his life around.

Each one of us has the opportunity – starting today – to reshape our lives, even to reinvent ourselves. Our lives are not predetermined by science, fate or divine will; we have God-given freedom, we can make real choices about our life, about who we want to be. We cannot necessarily determine our circumstances, but we can decide how to react to them. There are always choices to be made, options to be decided upon. We are authors of our own story, not mere victims of fortune.

Ultimately, Luke wanted his life to count for something. He didn't want to end up simply having visited this world. After decades of pastoral work, I have come to realise that it is not death as such that people fear most, or even the possibility of extinction, but the dread of insignificance: the idea that we will be born, live and one day die and none of it will matter. Something deep within us cries out against this. We feel there must be some purpose to our existence, some meaning that goes beyond 'Dave was here'.

At its best, religion helps to provide a sense of meaning by placing our lives within a greater purpose. However, it's important that religion isn't just escapism, or a set of simplistic answers to difficult questions. Certainty is the great danger, the great deception. But properly understood, religion is not about certainty; it's about faith, which is quite a different thing. After a lifetime of following Christianity and wrestling with matters of faith, I find my questions have not diminished, but rather increased. However, I have also come to realise that answers are hugely over-rated. Meaning in life does not derive from intellectual schemes and arguments, however persuasive; it's not about certainty.

But what, then, is it about? How do we discover meaning and significance to our lives? I would pinpoint four crucial factors: self-worth, personal authenticity, relationships, and a sense of purpose or vocation. None of these depends on faith for success; but for me, the Christian faith is fundamental to each one.

1. We have a fundamental need for self-worth

Sadly, religion doesn't always help with this. When the starting point is that we are miserable sinners, guilty before a judgemental God, it's hard to feel good about oneself. However, the fundamental message of Christianity is not human guilt, but divine grace – God's unconditional love for each of us.

This was illustrated to me recently when I talked with a grieving woman about her mother, whose funeral we were planning. I asked if there was a story or incident that illustrated or encapsulated what her mother was like. After a brief pause, she replied, 'When I was a small child, I broke a treasured vase, a family heirloom. Knowing how important it was, I screamed as it crashed to the floor and broke into a hundred pieces. But when my mother rushed into the room, she appeared relieved, not angry. Gathering me into her arms, she said, "Thank God! I thought you were hurt."' With tears in her eyes, the woman told me, 'That was what my mother was like. And that was the day I discovered that I was the family treasure.'

This is the heart of the Christian gospel: that you are the family treasure. God loves you more than anything you can do to stop God loving you. I believe that every child enters the world in a state of grace: with an openness and receptivity to divine love. Later experiences of rejection and fear choke this with feelings of guilt and failure when we get things wrong. Yet none of this alters the fact that we are loved and forgiven long before the 'vases' start crashing to the floor. Sure, there are things in each of our lives that need to change; things we may wish were different. We all need to grow and evolve. But it is love, not guilt, that brings this about.

The spiritual journey is in essence a longing to recover the primitive, childlike experience of grace: an intuition, an inner feeling of acceptance, the sense that God exists and that we are beloved of God, an awareness of the divine smile. This gives meaning and purpose to life, and breeds confidence that we can achieve something worthwhile.

2. We have a need for personal authenticity

Rabbi Zusha, the Hasidic teacher, once said, 'In the coming world, they will not ask me: "Why were you not Moses?" They will ask me: "Why were you not Zusha?"'

The problem is that it can take a long time to find out who we really are. It took me thirty years to even start to understand who I am. There is a wise old Quaker saying, 'Let your life speak.' But I was too busy listening to other voices to hear my own inner voice.

Of course, I was not unusual in this: most of us initially formulate our deepest truths and values from the ideas and example of people we admire and look up to. But there comes a time when we must stop being mere echoes of others and start to listen seriously to our own life, to become authentic.

The Quaker teacher Parker Palmer writes, 'Before you tell your life what truths and values you have decided to live up to, let your life tell you what truths you embody, what values you represent.'* In other words, trust the divine within yourself. By all means, admire and learn from God in others, but then discover the divine within yourself and be true to that.

Morality must not be reduced to a checklist cobbled together from the ideas of great people, or from the Bible, that we then try to emulate. A true sense of meaning in life develops when we discover the truths and values at the heart of our own God-given identity and honour them. Only in this way are we living our own life, not someone else's.

Personal authenticity means being true to yourself and to what you believe – in your relationships, in your business dealings, in your financial decisions, in the way you treat strangers and friends, in life's many choices and transactions. Meaning comes from living your own life, not someone else's, and living it with integrity, proud to be who you are in your deepest and truest self.

3. We have a need of relationships – to give and receive love

When I baptise a baby I always use a Celtic blessing that has the line, 'May you know what it is to love and be

---

* Parker J. Palmer, *Let Your Life Speak: Listening for the Voice of Vocation* (John Wiley & Sons, 1999).

loved.' Surely, there can be no greater wish for a child at the start of his or her life. Many rich and famous people leave this world friendless, miserable and frustrated, while others who possess very little depart in peace, surrounded by friends and loved ones, knowing that their lives have had significance.

Human beings are created to love and be loved. And experiencing this – whether in family relationships, marriage, partnership or friendship – is a central source of meaning to our existence. To discover love is to come home. It is where we came from and where we return to in our best moments.

As the philosopher Sam Keen points out, nothing dramatises the necessity and centrality of love in human life more than its absence. To the degree that we are haunted by feelings of abandonment, loneliness and emptiness, life becomes meaningless. We know that we ought to have loved and been loved better. And at the end of any addiction – to booze, cocaine, sex or success – 'we always discover that what we were blindly running after was love, and that all we ever caught was a poor substitute. And it didn't satisfy us because we can never get enough of what we didn't want in the first place.'*

---

* Sam Keen, *To Love and be Loved* (Bantam Books, 1999).

The need to give and receive love is written into our biological and spiritual DNA. The sense of meaning in our lives flourishes when we experience loving, reciprocal relationships. To be alone (not single), or to be in conflict, or to sense hatred is alien to everything we were made to be, which is why Jesus teaches us to love even our enemies. Hatred destroys any sense of meaning in life; love creates it.

One of my dearest friends and greatest heroes was Peter Thomson, an Australian Anglican priest who died a couple of years ago. Peter was (in the words of another friend) 'so warm you could toast yourself on him'. In his time, Peter was loved and respected by prime ministers, state premiers and leading figures in every walk of life. At his funeral, Tony Blair sent a message stating that Peter was one of the greatest people he had ever met. But Peter was precisely the same, whomever he was with. His oft-repeated maxim was that God is friendship, and he devoted his life to making friends with everyone because he believed that God was in everyone – 'even if you have to look a bit harder for him in some people!'

4. We have a need to contribute to the world

No one wants to be a mere passenger, or a consumer. We have a deep need to be contributors, to add something of worth to the world. But all too often, we have bought in to the mistaken idea that just a few chosen ones are the real contributors – people with some kind of vocation or calling – while the rest of us simply look on. The truth is that every single person has a vocation: a unique contribution to make to the enrichment of the world.

The first thing to say is that vocation is not necessarily the same as the job we do in order to earn our crust. Indeed, we are probably very lucky if the two coincide – though our vocation will invariably influence the way we do our job, whatever that may be.

The word 'vocation' is rooted in the Latin for 'voice'. But it doesn't come from a voice 'out there' calling us to be something we are not. It comes from a voice 'in here' calling us to be the person we were born to be, to fulfil the selfhood given to us at birth. Each person was created with a treasure, a gift of self that has the potential to develop into a unique passion or energy, which can contribute effectively to making the world a better place.

However, in families, schools, workplaces and churches, we are often trained away from our true selfhood towards images of acceptability. And we then live with increasing frustration because of the gap between who we truly are and who we feel we are supposed to be. Again, we end up living someone else's life instead of our own.

Jesus said, 'Unless you change and become like

children, you will never enter the kingdom of heaven.'* It is in childhood that we are most naturally receptive to divine grace; it is also in childhood that we are most in touch with our true selfhood. So we can glean important indications about our vocation from revisiting our childhood inclinations, passions and predispositions.

In my own childhood, I discovered that I liked to entertain people, to make them happy, to bring joy to the world. I later discovered that I was a leader, that I naturally formed gangs who joined me because of my relentless new ventures and ideas. I was an adventurer – but always in the company of others who became caught up with my escapades. In my late teens and early twenties I discovered that I loved to teach and influence people with ideas. But I grew up in an education system that never quite fitted me, and this fed a penchant for ideas that are novel, or even quirky, and for thinking outside the box.

So here I am, someone who loves to influence and inspire with ideas, who finds mainstream systems stuffy yet manages to hang into one, who enjoys being unconventional, who has a passion to bridge the gap between academia and popular thought and culture, who gathers

---

* Matthew 18:3.

people with a similar desire to make the world more stimulating, more inclusive, more fun.

These are the bones of my own vocational audit. I think I would be fundamentally the same if I were a college lecturer, a social worker, a CEO in a business, a dad (which I am), the manager of a charity shop, a sports coach, a pub landlord – or even a vicar! Some of these roles would no doubt fit me better than others, but what counts is finding expression for who I am, rather than the job or task through which I do it. This is what gives my life meaning.

So how about you? I wonder what the outline of your vocational audit might look like. For some people it will be striving for excellence or making the world a better place that will figure strongly; for some love and service of others will be central; for some achieving and making things happen; for others originality and creating beauty will be what matters; or attending to detail, or being inventive, or ensuring safety, or fighting for justice, or bringing peace and harmony, and so on. I encourage you to engage in your own vocational audit, thinking back to your childhood and youth, seeing what has been important to you over the years, recognising what has been stifled or frustrated.

Frederick Buechner wrote, 'The place God calls you to

is the place where your deep gladness and the world's deep hunger meet.'* It's a statement that starts with a legitimate emphasis on the self and moves towards the needs of the world, as does our fourfold recipe for a meaningful life:

Self-worth – learning to love myself.
Personal authenticity – learning to be myself.
Relationships – learning to give and receive love.
Vocation – learning to contribute to the world.

What sort of person do we wish to be? This is the real question behind religion, behind this book, behind life itself. It is basically the question that transformed Luke's life, which shifted him from a down-and-out existence on the streets to a life of self-esteem and productiveness. Jesus posed the question constantly, but especially in his story about a wise man who built his house on rock, and a foolish man who built his house on sand.

Who do we want to be?

What sort of life do we wish to have?

Jesus said, 'Follow me.'

---

* Frederick Buechner, *Beyond Words* (HarperSanFrancisco, 2004).

17. The last word

how to be a bad Christian

The chief thing that separates us from God is the thought that we are separated from God. If we get rid of that thought, our troubles will be greatly reduced.

– Father Thomas Keating

When Stefano first came to St Luke's, he didn't believe in God, but somewhere along the way he started calling himself a Christian.

Stef grew up in a working-class, atheist home in North London, in a distinctly socialist atmosphere. 'Politics, in particular socialism, is second nature to me,' he says. 'Even as a child I sensed the injustice and unfairness in the world.' His dad was a renowned photo-journalist who regaled the family with stories of wars and fighting and starving children. After studying politics at university, Stef too went on to become a photo-journalist.

He met Bernadette at university, and they moved into a house across the road from the church. And it was one Christmas morning, after their first two children came along, that the doors of the church began to open up for them. In the midst of unwrapping Christmas presents, Bernadette had a kind of epiphany. Knee deep in wrapping paper, she felt the number of toys and 'stuff' they had been given seemed obscene. As a lapsed Catholic, she felt Christmas must be about more than this. So she took the trip across the road and into St Luke's, where she was so impressed by the service and the community that she dashed home again, picked up her daughter and whisked her back to share the experience.

After this, Bernadette couldn't keep away from the place. She started taking both kids along, leaving Stef to meditate on the Sunday newspaper. But eventually a dilemma arose: when she was working and couldn't make it to church, the kids still wanted to go. So mum told them to ask the atheist in the house to take them – the one who didn't believe in going to church.

Not long after they had met, Stef had written a letter to Bernadette explaining that he wanted to believe in God but couldn't because of the bad things that happened to so many people. 'Humanity's problems would be solved by people not by some invisible Being,' he said. But now, faced with his own kids wanting to go to church, he felt it wouldn't be right to force his atheism on them – and maybe understanding Christianity might help them understand their own history and society. So he started taking them to church himself.

With the kids in the crèche or Sunday school, Stef would sit in the service. He did his best not to participate, but he got drawn in. St Luke's was a slightly irreverent, unpredictable community, which reminded him a little of the big, unruly family he had grown up in. After a while, he wanted to go to church himself rather than just take the kids.

'It wasn't that one week I was an atheist and the next I wasn't,' Stef says, 'but gradually I started to feel St Luke's was my home too and so I started to go up and receive Communion.' He even leads the prayers sometimes

– something he could never have dreamed of doing at one time.*

For years Stef gave church and religion a wide berth. He is not alone: most people in this country find church-going Christianity unappealing. This is a fact. Otherwise many more people would turn up at church on Sunday. Yet this widespread thumbs-down to formal religion is no indication of the true spiritual state of people today – as many of the stories in this book illustrate.

I don't believe God divides the world between Christians and non-Christians, believers and non-believers. God would need to be stupid to do this, and I don't believe God is stupid. God has to see past religious externals to look at what's going on in people's hearts. God must be more interested in the kind of people we are than in what we believe. There are people within all religious tradi-tions who treat others like dirt, who bully or kill in the name of God, and spread their 'gospel' of prejudice, bigotry and hate. And there are atheists, agnostics and people who just can't be bothered with religion, who give their lives in the service of others and look for all the world like followers of Jesus.

As Stef says, it wasn't a case of one minute he wasn't a

---

* Stef's story is taken from Martin Wroe, *The Gospel According to Everyone*.

Christian, the next he was. His spiritual journey went on for years – and still progresses today. The letter he wrote to Bernadette at university reveals a process of questioning that most people go through at some point, where perhaps we want to believe in God but find there are just too many things that don't seem to stack up.

I am a bad Christian. Far from having answers to all of life's hard questions, I have an ever-increasing list of these questions. Far from being an unwavering believer, I have frequent doubts. Far from being enamoured with everything in the Church and Christianity, I often despair of them. I hate the idea of being part of an exclusive club – the righteous ones! And I feel more at home in a pub with honest 'pagans' than I do in many churches.

But I am captivated by the figure of Jesus. I pointed out early on in the book that the original followers of Jesus were called 'people of the way' – folk who identified with the way of life that Jesus taught and demonstrated. I like this. I also like the fact that his first followers often behaved like a bunch of buffoons, that they misunderstood him, spoke out of turn, argued with each other, fell asleep when they should have been awake, basically kept on getting things wrong. But they continued following him. This gives me hope.

I have respect for all the faith traditions, and I have

dear friends of all faiths and none, but for me, Jesus Christ is the decisive revelation of God. The world continues to see many Christly figures, whom I admire greatly and try to emulate, but Jesus is, for me, the epiphany of what God is like – of God's character and passion. He is the one who gives shape and meaning to my world.

At the centre of Christ's message was the kingdom of God – a vision of what the world would be like if God were king instead of the authorities and politicians. It's a vision of justice, love and reconciliation, a culture of hope and freedom that I continually sign up for and try to represent.

If you like the sound of this . . .

If you share my faltering faith . . .

Congratulations!

You are a bad Christian!

Appendix 1
Spiritual practices

What are spiritual practices?

Life consists of two journeys: the outward journey of the body through time and space, and an inner journey of the soul. The outward journey creates the shell of our existence: where we live, what sort of work we do, whether or not we have a partner or children, what sort of things we spend our time on, all of which are very important aspects of our life. But the inner journey focuses on creating depth to our existence: discovering who we really are, establishing a sense of meaning and purpose to life, finding our moral and spiritual compass, deciding what it is that drives us.

Spiritual practices are deliberate actions or habits that cultivate the inner life. Every religion has its own tradition of practices based on its particular beliefs and rituals, but the aims are essentially the same: to quiet the mind, to help us connect with the divine, to nurture harmony between our beliefs and values and the commotion of everyday life.

We often bunch these practices together under the heading of 'prayer', but prayer can take many forms. To give a satisfactory catalogue of spiritual practices would require a book in itself, so I will simply outline three fundamental building blocks to spiritual practice.

Centred breathing

This exercise is a way of focusing attention inward and becoming grounded in the big picture of what life is about, rather than being lost in life's details. Spiritual development requires a greater awareness of what is going on inside us, and the ability to contextualise this within God's unconditional love. In my experience, a centring practice is essential to grasping the meaning of prayer. We can exercise it virtually anywhere: in the kitchen or the park, during a lunch break or on a bus or train, or before falling asleep at night (in fact, it will probably lead to a better night's sleep).

I learned the practice of centred breathing from my Enneagram teachers, Helen Palmer and David Daniels. This is more or less how they teach it.

1. Sit upright in a chair with your legs uncrossed and your feet on the floor. Close your eyes or relax your vision in a gentle gaze so as to turn your attention away from your surroundings.

2. Become aware of your breath, noticing its passage in and out. Let go of any other thoughts. However, don't worry if thoughts arise; gently set them aside and return your attention to your breathing, allowing your body to relax with the constant motion. Breath is always there in the present moment. And because it has no content or agenda of its own, it provides a wonderful neutral focus. It doesn't judge. It isn't anxious. It isn't concerned with what is going on around. It is just present all the time, constantly regenerating body and mind.

3. Follow each breath on its journey in and down. If you wish, place your hand on your tummy and feel it swell with each breath. Then feel it contract as the breath turns and you exhale. Very soon you feel grounded in your body, and this groundedness becomes the basis for being more receptive to yourself and others – and God.

4. Each time your attention shifts away from breathing to other thoughts, sensations or surrounding noises, allow yourself to be aware of them, then bring your attention back to the breath. In this calm state, you can become aware of your preoccupations and reactions, and begin to let them go.

211

5. At the end of the exercise, gently return your attention to the surroundings. Become aware of the chair, and the noises around you, and open your eyes.

If you wish, you can record these steps and listen to them as you practise. You can continue with the exercise as long as you wish, but try following it for ten or fifteen minutes. It may or may not include saying some specific prayers, or releasing concerns and anxieties. But the practice is an expression of prayer in itself.

Listening to silence

The Quakers make silence their central act of prayer and worship. They generally sit in quietness for an hour or so in their gatherings as a way of opening themselves to the inspiration of God's Spirit. Being silent is counter-intuitive in a cacophonous culture that demands constant stimulation, yet a short period of silence in a peaceful environment can be hugely rejuvenating. From time immemorial, people have discovered this as a way of reconnecting with what matters in life, with their deeper selves, with God.

Some people practise silence with their eyes closed to avoid distractions. Personally, I like to sit silently gazing out of a window. One of my favourite places to do this is on the first floor of our house looking at the birds bobbing around the tree outside. Many times, when inspiration has dried up while I try to write a sermon or a chapter of a book, a few coal tits, a robin and a goldfinch have come to the rescue. This too is a fundamental form of prayer.

There is no perfect time or place to be silent. Some may prefer to practise silence in the countryside, surrounded by the sounds of nature. Urbanites like me may find a busy street or a city park just as amenable. God's presence is everywhere. The spiritual practice of silence is simply the knack of quietly opening oneself to that divine presence, allowing anxiety to subside and becoming receptive to the energy of the Spirit.

Wakefulness – living in the moment

Contemporary living tends to push us into existing on autopilot; we often float across the surface of life without connecting in any meaningful way with people, events or the world around. Wakefulness or mindfulness is the practice of paying greater attention to the ordinary things of everyday life, of being present in the moment.

This can be difficult. Most of us have developed the habit of escaping the mundane by projecting our minds into the past or the future, or by distracting ourselves with the internet or TV or a computer game, etc. So we shouldn't expect too much of ourselves. I suggest beginning modestly: try devoting an hour here or there to practising being present in the moment. Have a lingering bath instead of a rushed shower. Enjoy the experience of a relaxed coffee in the garden instead of glugging it down and dashing off to the next activity. Consciously stop yourself from mentally flying off to what you will do tonight, or brooding over what you should have done or said yesterday. Little by little we can slow down and actually enjoy the mundane activities of life, as well as looking forward to pleasurable events later on.

For some people mindfulness is linked to more playful or creative activities such as drawing, playing with clay, singing or dancing. Rob Pepper, who provided the drawings for this book, has regularly held life-drawing classes at St Luke's, where the act of drawing is understood as a form of meditation in which participants can be fully present to that moment and the person or object being drawn.

Nowadays, mental health professionals recognise the benefits of mindfulness to people suffering from anxiety and depression. But it is also a form of prayer that can make us more susceptible to the divine presence.

Daily prayer

Many people have tried to practise daily prayer or meditation and failed miserably, mostly because they have set their expectations too high. Determining to spend an hour praying or meditating each morning, for example, is bound to fail. It's not by coincidence that we speak of 'practices', because spiritual exercise, like physical exercise, requires patient practice based on slow progress. And we need some assistance. We need to know where to begin.

The Irish Jesuit website, www.sacredspace.ie, is a pretty good place to begin. Here you will find a simple formula for daily prayer and reflection with various options to be explored. You could spend a few minutes there before going to work, or when you first sit at your desk, or at any other point during the day.

Beginning and ending the day with a simple prayer is another useful practice. The Serenity Prayer that I have recommended several times in this book is a great way to start the day:

> *God grant me the serenity*
> *to accept the things I cannot change;*
> *courage to change the things I can,*
> *and wisdom to know the difference.*

The New Zealand Prayer Book offers a prayer for the end of the day that breathes a wonderful, simple sense of closure before going to sleep:

> *It is night after a long day.*
> *What has been done has been done;*
> *what has not been done has not been done;*
> *let it be.*

Also, millions of people find short repetitive prayers through the day a great benefit. One of the most common is the Jesus Prayer that dates back to the desert monasteries of the fifth century:

> *Lord Jesus Christ, Son of God, have mercy on me, a sinner.*

Some people shorten the prayer to:

> *Lord Jesus, Son of God, have mercy.*

But you can compose your own prayer to repeat at different times during the day. For some people words are less helpful, so simple actions like fingering a rosary or lighting a candle prove more satisfying.

In France, the Taizé community has produced hundreds of repetitive prayers in the form of beautiful chants, which can be downloaded from iTunes.

Finally, it's worth noting the value of repetitive praying now recognised in the findings of neuroscience and cognitive psychology. Cognitive scientists now know that when we think the same thoughts over, we set up neural pathways in our brains. This is one way, at least, in which prayer can transform our thoughts and lives.

Appendix 2
The Enneagram

The Enneagram is a powerful and dynamic system that describes nine personality profiles – nine distinct and fundamentally different ways of thinking, feeling and acting. Drawing on ancient wisdom and modern psychological categories, the Enneagram offers incredibly useful insight for personal and spiritual development. I first encountered the system twelve years ago, and since then it has become indispensable, both in my personal life and in my work as a vicar.

Briefly, the Enneagram (*ennea* is Greek for 'nine', and *gram* is 'something written down') suggests that each of us has a central preoccupation or compulsion linked to our personality type, which causes us to search for certain things in life and avoid others. When we are running on automatic pilot this preoccupation is where our attention goes, and it has both positive and negative sides to it. But being our default mode, we are mostly unconscious of it.

At the risk of oversimplifying, I will give a thumbnail sketch of the nine personality profiles. Hopefully this brief description will whet your appetite to explore the system more fully.

Type One: the Perfectionist

These are responsible, independent, hard-working people with high standards and principles. They can come across as critical and nit-picky, but they are also very hard on themselves, seldom living up to their own expectations, rarely managing to placate their strident inner critic. The attention of Ones naturally goes to spotting what's wrong, and what needs to be done to get it right. They excel with detail.

Type Two: the Helper

Spending their lives attending to other people's needs, Twos are cheerful, outgoing, warm and personable with a relentless knack of sensing what the rest of us want or need – perhaps before we realise it ourselves. However, this can lead to Twos being manipulative. Also, since they prefer giving to receiving, they often struggle to acknowledge their own needs or ask for help from others.

Type Three: the Achiever

Self-confident, ambitious and successful, Threes have boundless energy to pursue their goals and projects. They are born winners and great motivators. But, chameleon-like, they often change their image to suit the situation or to gain approval. They may also come across as unfeeling and calculating when single-mindedly pursuing their latest project.

Type Four: the Romantic

Fours detest mediocrity and are drawn to the extremes of emotional experience. Often melancholic, they spend their lives searching for the significant and meaningful, or for that 'something' they sense is missing. They generally have a distinct aesthetic sensibility and, though caught up in their own emotions, can be wonderfully empathetic in emotionally painful situations.

Type Five: the Observer

These are the most private types, who need their own time and space to recharge their batteries. They may come across as detached, especially emotionally, observing rather than engaging. The mind is where Fives feel most comfortable, and they make fine thinkers and analysts who have a love of information and knowledge, often in specialised areas of interest or study. They are self-sufficient and like predictable routines, but they make creative intellectuals.

Type Six: the Loyal Sceptic

If something can go wrong, the Six will probably have spotted it, because their attention naturally goes to possible hazards and threats, or to ulterior motives in people. On the other hand, they are inquisitive and make excellent critical thinkers. Instinctively suspicious of authority figures and overly successful people, they readily align themselves with underdog causes. Yet once you gain their trust, Sixes are deeply loyal and committed friends and colleagues.

Type Seven: the Epicure

Pleasure is very important to these types: they can achieve almost anything and work from dawn till dusk, provided it feels like fun. Sevens are life's optimists. They are charming, upbeat and adventurous. However, their tendency is to avoid the darker side of life. And if their interest isn't maintained, they drop out or switch off, with their minds shifting to more pleasurable options. Naturally unconventional, with fast minds, they make great lateral thinkers.

Type Eight: the Protector

These are the most assertive or aggressive personality types, with an all-or-nothing approach to life. Fiercely independent, Eights are natural leaders with a great sense of fairness and justice. They will go to any lengths to protect their loved ones and those in their care, or to pursue a cause they believe in. Yet people often find the passion of an Eight overpowering: Eights never do anything by halves, from drinking with friends to a theological debate. Passion is their lifeblood.

Type Nine: the Mediator

No one can take in and understand the views of a group of people better than a Nine. However, they are not so good at determining their own views, or identifying what it is that they want. Peace and harmony is the name of the game for these types, and they will often go along with other people's agendas to keep the peace. But when the feeling of being pressurised becomes too much, the buried anger emerges in stubbornness and passive aggression. Nines make excellent arbitrators and lovely partners (I know – I have one).

Even though I have described something of the behaviours associated with each of the nine types, it is important to stress that Enneagram typology is less about the behaviours and more about the motives, spiritual energies and worldview of the nine personalities. People may behave in very similar ways but for very different reasons.

Simply understanding ourselves better is a potentially huge boost to spiritual development, but the many different layers and aspects of the Enneagram system have made it a phenomenally useful tool for anyone seeking a deeper spirituality. It also offers great insight into the dynamics of intimate and work-related relationships.

If you want to know more about the Enneagram, you could check out the following:

- My website has more details about the system, a blog and information about my programme of Enneagram workshops: www.davetomlinson.co.uk.

- Look at the website of Enneagram Worldwide (the organisation with whom I am a certified Enneagram teacher), which contains many helpful resources: www.enneagramworldwide.com.

- *The Essential Enneagram* by David Daniels is an excellent, concise introduction to the Enneagram that includes a personality test.

- Download the app 'Know Your Type' from the iTunes app store. This is easily the best Enneagram app with lots of interesting resources, including a 'Find your type' section.

Appendix 3
Useful websites

Support social justice

www.one.org – a grassroots campaign to end poverty and preventable disease, especially in Africa.

www.amostrust.org – a small but effective charity run by friends of mine who promote justice and hope for forgotten communities and support peacemakers in Palestine/Israel.

www.quaker.org/faith-action – links to information about the different Quaker social justice projects ongoing, and how to get involved.

www.centreforsocialjustice.org.uk – an independent, charitable think tank working to 'reverse social breakdown' in the UK.

Volunteer time

www.timebank.org.uk – a national volunteering charity that links you up to local projects that need help, including youth mentoring schemes. Just fill in your postcode and see what's happening near you.

www.do-it.org.uk – a really comprehensive database of

volunteering projects that lets you search by a whole pile of variables including sector, target group, time of day you want to work, etc.

www.csv.org.uk – another well-established, national volunteering charity that offers training and signposts to opportunities.

www.vso.org.uk – very well-known and trusted initiative with a wide range of opportunities around the world.

www.msf.org.uk – a humanitarian medical charity (Doctors Without Borders) working overseas. You don't need to be a doctor or nurse to get involved.

Live generously

www.generous.org.uk – an initiative that encourages us to do a little more a little more often to make shared life on our planet sustainable and more bearable for as many people as possible. Get lots of ideas for living generously and add a few of your own.

www.randomactsofkindness.org – lots of ideas, resources, stories and links inspiring us to practise kindness and pass it on to others.

www.charterforcompassion.org – an initiative aimed at restoring compassion to the centre of religious and ethical life. Sign the charter, make a commitment, join the online community and spread the word.

Shop ethically

www.ethicalconsumer.org – aiming to make global businesses more sustainable through consumer pressure, this website offers a database of research on company behaviour against 23 ethical criteria, and offers comprehensive guidance to financial and shopping decisions.

www.fairtrade.org.uk – the site of the independent organisation that licenses use of the FAIRTRADE MARK on products in the UK.

www.traidcraft.co.uk – a Christian-based organisation that fights poverty through trade by ensuring that the suppliers of goods are given a fair deal and that the environment is respected.

Make peace

www.stethelburgas.org – a peacemaking centre based in a restored church building destroyed by an IRA bomb in 1993. St Ethelburga's Centre for Reconciliation and Peace runs dialogue facilitation courses, meditation sessions, multi-faith platforms and online resources, etc.

www.religionsforpeace.org – the largest international religious coalition dedicated to promoting peace. Lots of downloadable resources and videos about peacemaking.

Do you wish this wasn't the end?
Are you hungry for more great teaching, inspiring
testimonies, ideas to challenge your faith?

Join us at www.hodderfaith.com, follow us on Twitter
or find us on Facebook to make sure you get the latest from
your favourite authors.

Including interviews, videos, articles, competitions
and opportunities to tell us just what you thought about
our latest releases.

www.hodderfaith.com

 HodderFaith

 @HodderFaith

 HodderFaithVideo

HODDER
WHERE FAITH IS INSPIRED